The Primacy of Love

THE PRIMACY OF LOVE

by DR. AUGUST ADAM

Translated from the German by

ELISABETHE CORATHIEL NOONAN

The Newman Press · Westminster, Maryland

Nihil Obstat: JOANNES M. T. BARTON, S.T.D., L.S.S.,
Censor Deputatus.

Imprimatur: E. MORROGH BERNARD, VIC. GEN.
Westmonasterii, die 14a Novembris, 1955.

This is a translation of *Der Primat der Liebe* published in 1954 by Butzon & Bercker of Kevelaer in West Germany

Library of Congress Catalog Card Number: 58-8756
Printed in the United States of America

Contents

Foreword

THE dual meaning of the word, morality, which in the popular mind has tended to become more and more confused and identified with questions of sexual behavior, is nowadays acknowledged in ethics and by teachers as an established fact and no longer treated with reservations. The learned have accepted the word as it is used in common currency and adapted themselves to the vulgar viewpoint. In examining a large number of old and newer works of pulpit oratory, the writer realized that this present-day use of the word morality was quite unknown to preachers in earlier times. In fact, it has only been applied in this sense from the pulpit in our own lifetime, during the last few decades. This discovery forced on him the urgent need to examine what justification there might be for limiting the concept of morality in this way.

The results of this examination will be found in the present volume, which is by no means designed to lessen the importance of sex, but rather to put it in its proper place amid the structure of public order and propriety. Christ expressly specified love as the most important of all Christian virtues. In a classification in which love is the chief commandment, chastity loses nothing—indeed it increases in importance, while overemphasis on sex does far more to endanger sexual morality than to further it.

The author intended his thoughts on this subject to be primarily helpful to his brother-priests in their labors for the care of souls, though he by no means rules out the possibility that they may prove serviceable in other learned circles, where he trusts they will be taken seriously. His spiritual director and guide in this exposition, as well as in the critical judgment he has brought to bear on his studies, was the Prince of Catholic theologians, St. Thomas Aquinas.

May these writings bring inspiration and help to a great many preachers and teachers!

AUGUST ADAM.

Straubing,
November 1, 1947.

In this new edition only a few unimportant changes have been made. The book has meanwhile appeared in the Dutch, Portuguese and—partly—Flemish languages.

THE AUTHOR.

Straubing,
May 1, 1954.

THE PUBLISHERS gratefully acknowledge permission to include excerpts from the following works:

Hymns to the Church by Gertrude von Le Fort, translated into English by Margaret Chanler, published by Sheed & Ward, New York.

Orthodoxy by G. K. Chesterton. Copyright © 1908, 1935, by G K. Chesterton. Reprinted by permission of Dodd, Mead & Company.

The Primacy of Love

CHAPTER 1

Fundamental Questions

THE rise of a race is primarily conditioned by its morality and the conservation of its inner strength. This historical fact is once again receiving the recognition it deserves, after a period of materialism in which it tended to be overlooked. Propaganda glorifying family life, stimulating the national desire for health and fitness, and underlining the love and care of children, is on the increase. It runs parallel with efforts to uproot disruptive elements in our cultural life which have all too long aimed at casting doubt on the ideals of chastity and matrimonial fidelity. All these efforts for the moral improvement of the masses not only deserve our interest but demand our cooperation. The obligation rests on us not merely because of our duty as good citizens; it is also a religious responsibility.

Practicing Catholics have the good fortune to possess the unquestionable truth which is made available to them in divine revelation transmitted through the teachings of the Church. They are therefore quite secure from dangerous errors that may creep in through doubts on fundamental questions of belief and morality. They do not need to cast sheep's eyes in the direction of ancient and modern philosophers for guidance and wisdom which is worldly wise, therefore quite unstable, the only dependable thing about it being its liability to change from age to age. Maybe there are some people who throw away this great good fortune, some who consider it historically more proper to search for truth in preference to recognizing that the thing they are looking for is already in their possession. There will always be some with an urge to fight, people who would rather strain themselves in a vain struggle than accept truth gracefully, secure in the knowledge that it is theirs without the need of conquest. But of course, we must not forget two factors which are easily overlooked. In the first place it requires, on the whole, more heroism to accept truth than to cast doubt on it. Truth can be hard and bitter, which is why people have at all times preferred crucifying it to worshipping it. And secondly—a thing we Catholics are also often inclined to lose sight of—truth is not only a free gift, but also a sacred trust. We, too, even when we have genuine faith, are not exempt from the command to "hunger and thirst after righteousness" which our Lord numbered among the Beatitudes. The blessed heritage of faith, which has come down to us in a living stream from the apostles century after century, must be discovered and accepted anew by every individual before it can be taken up as a personal possession. The poet's words, "That which you have inherited from your forefathers, win it, in order that you may enjoy it," applies more to the heritage of faith than to any other heirloom. The true believer is the receiving instrument of eternal truth; all the experience of two centuries is at his service. But he must be "tuned in"; and he must also transmit. The Gospel which once, like leavened dough, acted from within upon a whole world of antique culture, renewing and changing it completely, is now in his possession. It is his duty to carry it into his environment so that it may once again perform its regenerative function. We are the people, each and every one of us individually, in whom the eternal truth must stand revealed. Woe unto us if our precious heritage becomes merely a buried treasure, eking out an anemic existence as a half-dead letter in printed books and never penetrating our understanding as a thing more vital than a mere intellectual concept! We dare not allow any difficulty to prevent us from sharing this truth with others, by our actual living example—sharing it with that benighted world around us which thirsts for truth just as ardently as it appears to abhor it. The spirit of truth, when it becomes a living reality in the practicing Christian, will "convince the world of sin and of injustice and of judgment" (John 16: 8). For two thousand years divine truth has been made flesh and dwelt among us—and yet there are so many men, even men of good will and noble intentions, who do not know it. Are not we, who should be witnesses of truth, responsible for withholding it from them? All around us, among those with whom we have daily contact, we meet with prejudice against the faith and against Catholic morality. But are we not ourselves to blame, we who possess the truth and have failed to make ourselves living examples of it? We who affirm the truth with our lips but so often by our acts deny it?

No doubt the imperfection of human nature is at the root of much that obscures the full radiance of truth in the weaker members of Christ's Church. As long as this earthly pilgrimage lasts, there will be this human weakness. It belongs to the very nature of the Church, the mystical body of God-made-man who took our imperfections upon Him in order that He might redeem them. Already in the very earliest days of Christianity, the Church found it necessary to conduct campaigns of reformation, sifting out the dross. Able men like Tertullian, fanatical innovators like Novatian, had perforce to be expelled from the "community of the blessed." Christ Himself said there would always be tares among the good grain and there will be scandalous and disturbing elements within the Church until, at the end of time, the City of God stands revealed in all its bliss and beauty.

But a far greater menace than human weakness to the dynamic power of truth often proceeds from the very men whose duty it is to give instruction. Instead of fulfilling their task conscientiously, they allow their utterances to be colored by passing fashions in thought. They get carried away by their own pet fancies and slip in interpretations which seem to them more suitable to current conditions than the sober phrases of sound dogma and morality. And that is how misshapen, heretical conceptions find their way into the religious mentality of the people. If the Catholic Church from the very start had proceeded even more drastically than it did against the slightest deviation, it could not have been accused of either fanaticism or intolerance, not even if it had punished the offenders more severely than murderers or adulterers. For the slightest deviation from the straight line of divine revelation leads to fundamental confusion, a departure from truth which, insignificant as it may appear at the beginning, must lead eventually to a radical disturbance in the Christian community. If a traveler unconsciously strays ever so little from the right path, every step will take him farther and farther from the way he should go until, in the end, he entirely loses his bearings. Priests and preachers are products of their times and therefore subject, like everyone else, to contemporary influences. They are always liable to confuse passing modes of thought with the eternal verities of divine revelation unless they keep to their course—

plotting it as carefully as the mariner does by the stars. This can only be done by checking back, by holding on steadfastly to the guidance of truth as revealed in the Scriptures and endorsed by the Holy Church.

In the following chapters, the author will rally all Catholic priests and preachers of truth to a serious examination of conscience on the question which strikes at the very root of all moral thought and behavior, namely: "What actually do we mean by morality?" If this question gives rise to smiles, let us recall that very often things which seem quite self-evident are the very ones which lie wide open to error, just because we consider it superfluous to waste any deeper thought upon them. Through no fault of ours, but certainly without any protest on our part, a universal moral concept has established itself during the last few decades, even in Catholic circles, which is in complete contradiction to our faith. The propagation of this concept is so menacing to true morality that even our own preachers and theologians have occasionally been led to quite dangerous conclusions by it. And though in the meantime, at least in leading theological circles, the situation has eased, there is almost as much danger of the other extreme (a too broad-minded tolerance in place of the former strictness) setting in with regard to sex. In current colloquial speech there is still great danger from the false definition which makes not only the man in the street but even the trained lawyer employ the words "moral—immoral" as if they had no other application than to sex. Of course, we cannot in a work of the present scope penetrate deeply into the original definition of morality as a concept. The early Christian maxim that it is better to have true piety than to be able to explain exactly what piety is, applies also to morality. We are not concerned here with dull book learning or pedantry, but with the orientation of warm, pulsating life in its relation to eternal principles of the living truth of Jesus Christ and His Church. A heavy responsibility rests on the promulgators of divine truth. They have to explain this truth without the least abridgment or addition, without compromise and without concession to any passing opinion; but also without yielding in the least to any pet theories they themselves may have conceived. We who preach must meditate on the law by day and night (cf. Ps. 1: 2), must check our sermons constantly by divine revelation in order to avoid the danger of current catchwords and modish forms that look deceptively like hallowed traditions but prove, on examination, to have been born yesterday. It is so easy to confuse that which goes down well with contemporary audiences as a heaven-sent solution quite measuring up to the eternal verities.

Of course, the Catholic clergy may justly claim always to be in the forefront of those brave upholders of Christian principles who have fought for public order and good morals. Nor need they drop their eyes in shame if, occasionally, one of their number, weaker than the rest, has fallen by the way and given cause for disquiet among his people. Such an exception by no means disproves the rule that the great majority of the Catholic clergy are as honestly and earnestly occupied in practicing what they preach as any of their most upright Protestant colleagues can be. There were times, and precisely during the pious Middle Ages, when the moral untouchability of the clergy could be more easily disputed. But this does not release us from the obligation of asking ourselves whether we have constantly fulfilled our duty toward the souls entrusted to our care in this struggle. It is a fact that, taken all in all, we have little enough result to show for this struggle. It is a fact that the struggle itself has been wholly a defensive one. We have been handing out warnings about the movies and the theater, about fashions and about dancing, about degenerate art and literature; but we have not succeeded in winning over modern culture as a means of expression to the positive service of Christian betterment. As a censor and a knowledgeable expert on questions of what is right and proper, the clergyman, whether Catholic or Protestant, is, in the main, suspect, even in really devout circles. Now it is all very well to explain away all these facts by recalling the sophistication and unbelief of the modern world, to make bitter remarks about a degenerate age, and to comfort oneself with recollections of the voice in the wilderness. All this is a great sop to one's conscience and may send us on our way completely satisfied that we have done our best in the fulfillment of our duty. But we should have humility enough to turn the picture around and take a look at the other side. We are answerable to our own conscience and to God, and we should ask ourselves whether the fault may not, to some extent at least, lie at our own door. Have we perhaps, here and there, employed weapons that were less than sharp, in fact positively blunted? These truths of ours, that we have offered from the pulpit, have they indeed been God's truths? Have we allowed the dust of centuries to settle on our principles, so that their original brilliance no longer came through? Maybe our strategy needed overhauling—maybe the words "In that day some priests fell in battle, while, desiring to do so manfully, they went out unadvisedly to fight" (I Mach. 5: 67) could with justice be applied to our method of waging battle, too.

Damaging results may ensue, not only from laxity and indifference, but also from clumsy and unwise tactics. Our pure and holy cause may find its driving force exhausted in the very tension of the preliminary approach when it comes up against the widespread conviction of the uselessness of getting out of step with the spirit of the age. And the writer is not merely alluding to ill-judged utterances some well-meaning priests may allow themselves to be betrayed into when carried away by their emotions. An inadequately prepared, too personal attack is just the kind of thing a chorus of opponents will welcome because it gives them an excuse to cry "prudery" and "fanaticism" and reduces the whole transaction to an absurdity. No, the fault may go far deeper. Defeat may be due to the false strategy of bringing big guns to bear on side issues, leaving the decisive point exposed to the enemy.

The possibility of a deviation from doctrine not only in individual instances but also in much wider spheres is by no means incompatible with the infallibility of the Church. History can supply many examples proving that such deviations do now and then occur. The objective infallibility of the Church does not entail the subjective infallibility of all its members. Unquestioning reliance on the authority of the Church must not therefore lead Catholics, even priests, to the conclusion that their own answers to the burning questions of the age are equally equipped with the charism of infallibility, even when offered in good faith. Ethically, as well as dogmatically, such self-satisfaction would be very debatable, and the danger of it is increased rather than diminished by the fact of the error being an unconscious one, since it appears to him who commits it simply an expression of superior faith.

Certainly the Church, directly inspired by the Holy Ghost, is infallible. The sacred college upholds the purity of its objective teaching and guards it against error; pastoral direction looks after the practical application of that teaching and its working out in the day-by-day religious and moral life of the faithful. Willing acceptance of this pastoral ruling only now and then involves sacrifice on the part of an individual Catholic, perhaps in a religious crisis or in certain specific situations. Normally, every Catholic accepts the ruling as a foregone conclusion and a self-evident part of his existence. But this acceptance is entirely passive and by no means constitutes living faith in its entirety. Rather it is the necessary preliminary, the groundwork or skeleton of faith. To turn these eternal verities into reality in our daily life, translating them into flesh and blood by all our thought and all our actions, is our one and only purpose here on earth. "The just man liveth by faith" (Rom. 1: 17; Gal. 3: 11; Heb. 10: 38). This faith calls for more than an automatic readiness to accept the dogmas of the Church, which are really nothing more than the signposts, the very alphabet of belief. Not until we apply them to life itself do they show us the way to truth and right living. To explain revealed truth is the Church's part; but the application of truth is the task of every individual Christian and this responsibility cannot be delegated to anyone else. Of course, the pastoral authority also guides the individual in his undertaking—but it cannot possibly go into such minute detail as to rule out any further need for subjective reasoning. Encyclicals, pastoral letters, and the counsel of a confessor can never treat a problem or question so exhaustively as to leave no more room for the exercise of individual conscience. In the end, every man must face the Supreme Judge in his own person.

For the nearness of men is like flowers
withering on graves,

And all comfort is like a voice
from without.—
But you are a voice in the inmost soul.
—Gertrud von Le Fort,
"Hymns to the Church."

Quite a number of human factors enter into the personal acceptance of dogmas and their application to our daily life. There may even be an innocent lack of clear understanding, or of judgment, in which individual leanings, education, emotional stresses, and other circumstances play an important part. Here at once we may perceive a breach in the defenses through which error may creep like a thief in the night; for the charism of infallibility belongs only to the Church and its sacred college. With the greatest desire to be a true believer, an individual Catholic may still have errors on his conscience. In theology, these errors are known as heresy. Quite wrongly, heresy is commonly believed to be of rare occurrence. Actually, it is more widespread than one would suppose, and not even among individuals but among whole schools of thought and even in learned circles. That these have often been infected we have ample proof; we need only recall the witch hunts of old. The errors of bygone days are by no means vanished curiosities, mere museum pieces. The Church has certainly branded them so that they may be clearly recognizable, but they have by no means shed that misleading magic which centuries ago made them so perilous, even to orthodox thought. They are like will-o'-the-wisps that tempt wanderers into the wilderness—errors that are ever again committed, not only by avowed heretics, but also by faithful Catholics who fail to recognize them for what they are.

Ever and anon old heresies reappear, in different

forms and under new names, as often as the age produces a spiritual background similar to that from which they first arose. Monophysitism, which recognizes only the divine in Jesus Christ, is still kept alive today in the prayers of many of the faithful; so is Pelagianism in the striving for perfection, Novatianism in the desire for exclusiveness, Montanism in the yearning for supernatural visions and extraordinary grace. Let the dogmaticians hunt these heresies as ardently as they please, what will it avail, so long as pastoral theology tolerates them and gives them foothold?

Another far-reaching misconception lies in the belief that deviation from subjective faith occurs only among negligent and lukewarm Christians. People forget that there are two kinds of errors: errors of defect which spring from unbelief, and errors of excess which have the opposite origin. While the first kind express themselves in lukewarmness, indifference, faultfinding, worldliness; the signs by which we may recognize the mystical group are subjectivity and fanaticism, an uncritical acceptance and desire for so-called "wonders," and a self-conceit which is impatient of authority, frequently claiming direct spiritual illumination. Overemphatic outward piety, self-satisfaction and contempt for other people are qualities that often go with the second class of error.[1]

We have fallen into the habit of regarding rationalistic unbelief as the most dangerous enemy because it simply denies. But the unbalanced excesses of mysticism and rigorism have much in common with the more easily recognized errors. Ecclesiastical history provides ample proof that the swing of the pendulum in the opposite direction often did the Church more harm than the actual falling from grace of which it was the recoil. Whenever it went so far as to end in separation from the Church, the consequent enmity was far greater and more fanatic than that of the lapse against which it rebelled. The Monophysites, for instance, attacked "unbelieving" Catholics, not merely with spiritual weapons, but also with fire and the sword; and the Albigensian rebellion became so menacing that Crusaders had to be employed to put it down.

There is still more danger in the fact that such a spirit may penetrate deeply into the Church itself and draw even religious circles into its orbit. Fanaticism in favor of an inflated cause is fond of hiding under the mantle of exceptional zeal. It then becomes more pontifical than the pope and is very ready with the retort of "laxity" when directed back to the royal highway which deviates neither to the right nor to the left. Earnestly devout but unenlightened souls may very easily fail to detect the error. A classical example of mass contamination was the witch-hunting mania which swept even the most conscientious off their feet and proved by its widespread ramifications and long duration that not only isolated mentalities are liable to be infected. It can become a real epidemic and affect a whole generation. The noble-minded Friedrich von Spee required courage of no mean order to fly in the face of the accepted convention of his times by denouncing the evil. It is shattering to read some of the passages of his *Cautio criminalis* in which he demonstrates to his contemporaries the senselessness of proceedings which completely contradict Christianity and common sense while masquerading as very particular manifestations of faith. Instead of having Catholic public opinion on his side, von Spee was surrounded by critics, the majority of them well-educated, pious people who had been carried away by their belief in devils and had allowed the far more important truths of Christianity to be pushed into the background. Von Spee is constantly having to defend himself against charges of wavering faith. In his very first chapter, he writes: "If a man is seized with eagerness to proceed against witchcraft he would be well advised to control himself, adding to his zeal some reflection and wisdom, which he may not possess. Precipitation does not always spring from virtue; far more often it is a purely natural urge. Virtue on the other hand is modest and temperate; it is open to conviction and not the less valuable for being circumspect." A similar overemphasis on one aspect of truth at the expense of others was responsible for starting campaigns against heretics in the Middle Ages, not least among them the celebrated case of Galileo. Indeed, most of the confusions of Christian thought, which are nowadays so welcome to the Church's opponents, spring from this same misplacement of emphasis. It might be a rewarding task for our apologetics to examine more deeply the causes of such errors, setting down the conclusions arrived at without false tenderness to any seemingly hallowed traditions. Perhaps God is actually forcing this overdue task upon us through the pressures of our enemies. All the dark shadows which seek to disfigure the fair face of the Bride of Jesus Christ before the oft-quoted forum of history have their origin in that exaggeration which is not a denial of Christian truth but which throws it out of balance. And all this comes about because the same energy with which rationalism is automatically countered is seldom brought to bear upon its opposite, sentimental mysticism.

None of these deviations, however, has succeeded in casting a shadow of doubt upon a single dogma. Not even the most fanatic adherents of the witch hunt ever dreamed of attacking the moral principles of love and justice theoretically, much as they befogged the concept of them in their practical dealings, thus preventing all moderating factors from coming into play. Which proves the point made on a previous page, namely, that a truth may be set down in all the catechisms in the world but still have no influence whatever on the building up of conscience unless diocesan leadership takes active steps to ensure that erroneous thought-tendencies and prejudices are countered from the start, and the whole teaching of faith and morality accentuated with equal emphasis. Errors of the past force us to ask ourselves conscientiously whether similar distortions are possible, and perhaps even taking place, at the present time. Every period has its own special problems, its particular ailments; and our own times cannot claim the privilege of being entirely exempt from them.

The examples given also prove that not only laymen but priests also are liable to place a false emphasis on one or other article of the Catholic faith. One might almost say that the professional theologian is even more prone to this failing than the ordinary Catholic believer who gives himself wholeheartedly to his faith and thus very often finds the right road automatically in cases of doubt; whereas the learned professional, primed with all the distinctions, very often cannot see the woods for trees. Moreover, we must emphasize that there is a great risk of unwelcome deviationism when popular questions of the day are occasions for polemical invective. Another peril arises when the denial of truth through heresy forces the defender of the faith to underline one doctrine more emphatically than another. Polemics have always been doubtful counselors for a troubled conscience and have led more than one fighter in God's cause to lose all in the heat of battle by disregarding the kernel of truth in the opponent's argument. (And whoever heard of an error that did not contain at least a grain of truth?)

Catholic truth is more than the sum total of its doctrines. *Veritas una!* The phrase applies in the strictest sense. There is only one truth and it is indivisible and eternal, for it is identical with God Himself. O *æterna veritas et vera caritas et cara æternitas* (St. Augustine *Conf.*). O eternal truth and true love and dear eternity! As long as our consciousness is made up of parts, one impression at a time, we can perceive the unity of absolute truth only "through a glass in a dark manner" (I Cor. 13: 12). The object is clear and sharply defined, but the instrument through which we view it is out of focus and only a small part of this eternal infinity can be taken in—never the full grandeur of the whole. Never, as long as we are in mortal flesh, will the full glory of absolute truth be visible to us; our eyes can only catch a fleeting glimpse of a ray or two. We speak of separate truths, forgetting that this word must always be *singulare tantum.* All the truths of revelation are but parts, transmitted rays of the one, whole, indivisible, eternal truth. Our unenlightened natural intellect only too gladly absorbs these parts, tearing them out of their context, in which alone they make sense. Thus, often enough, truth turns into error; justice can become the greatest injustice when it degenerates into a "Shylock's bond," framed from self-seeking motives and completely out of tune with the eternal principles of right and wrong. The very word heresy (*hæresis*—choice) explains itself. On the preference for one truth at the expense of another, the whole of heresy is based.

Of course, falsehood can never take deep root, not only because of the vigilance of the sacred college, but also because the Catholic conscience knows its own limitations and is fully aware of its need for spiritual guidance. "Blessed are they that have not seen and have believed" (John 20: 29). This willing faith, completely content to abandon speculation but utterly ready here on earth to yield itself humbly and gladly to God's word, comes quite naturally to a Catholic; but it stands him in better stead where questions of faith are concerned than in matters involving moral judgment. The latter demand reflection, daily and hourly, for it is the Christian's duty to apply the commandments that have been imprinted on his conscience to the ordinary affairs of daily life, turning them to concrete reality; and this calls for the exercise of his own will and reason. In the moral sphere, a person feels mentally much more at home than in the dogmatic sphere. But this can become dangerous when a man grows so enamored of his own reasoning powers that he sees no necessity for checking with dogma at all. Today we are able to recognize clearly, for instance, that the overrigorous routine and asceticism of the early oriental monastic orders had more in common with the Stoical and Neoplatonic schools of thought than with the Gospels; but these early monks, who submitted to their self-imposed privations with such holy zeal and genuine striving for perfection, were quite ignorant of their origin. They found suitable texts to justify their systems of conduct, and would have been most upset if anyone had pointed out the error of their ways. St. Augustine met with the stoutest resistance, precisely from these earnest monks, when he formulated his comprehensive rule based entirely on the Gospel, and set about establishing it in monastic life.[2]

The challenge calling Catholics to more active cooperation—strengthened as it has been by the campaign against *sola fides* teaching—has led many, both priests and laymen, into mistaken ideas borrowed from Kant's philosophy and passing as true Christian thought. It would never occur to any Catholic to attempt to penetrate the mystery of the Trinity or of the Holy Eucharist by means of his own human reason. But it is quite common even for pious people and true believers to feel that they can decide moral issues on the basis of their own judgment and experience, especially when the verdict happens to be harsh and therefore appears to them particularly edifying. Should anyone venture to point out a slight discrepancy between their procedure and the truth, they are ready with glib references to tradition and practice, by which means they make short work of objections. Friedrich von Spee, in his campaign against witch-hunting, found this trick on the part of his opponents one of the most worrying problems he had to deal with. Again and again he laments that his intervention to prevent unjust proceedings was usually categorically swept aside because "in practice" the witch hunts had proved their efficacy.[3] *Hodie praxis*—and this neat phrase was regarded as adequate to remove all objection, disarm all criticism. Whoever dares to say a word against established practice falls foul of hallowed tradition and this can, in certain circumstances, expose him to sterner anathemas than if he had called into question one of the divine revelations. Catholics naturally respect tradition as a source of truth, but they should take care to distinguish genuine traditions that have come down century after century through the ancient Church from half-baked ideas that have wormed their way into the public conscience and are nothing more than sources of error and confusion.

Of all the ideas that can become a menace to the earnest believer, Manicheism is the one that has been most obstinately persistent. It has so many points of similarity with Christian teaching that theologians as well as laymen have been deceived by it. With its emphasis on strict morality—not omitting a contemptuous sidelong look at the laxity which sees no evil in nature and the human body—with its many ideals, so acceptable to Christian requirements; and with its glamorous spiritual aspirations, which succeeded in bemusing even Plato and St. Augustine; and especially with its sharp condemnation of contemporary degeneracy, "the debasing of all standards," no wonder preachers and theologians did not immediately recognize the false god of Manicheism, because he appeared to them as an angel of light. Pieper [4] calls Manicheism "an apparently indestructible outlook." "Only blindness could fail to see that the contempt in which Manicheism holds sexual relationship for the purpose of race-renewal has colored the traditional Christian concept of virtue, and especially of chastity. It is not perhaps a formulated opinion, but it certainly expresses itself in an unspoken attitude," says Pieper. It would almost seem—and indeed Pieper alludes to this [5]—as if the African Tertullian, who was expelled from the early Christian community for his excessive emphasis on the Sixth Commandment, had been brought back with honor in many a pulpit. No Catholic and certainly no priest would ever dream of casting aspersions upon the Church's teachings. But, when carried away by ill-considered enthusiasm, many may be in danger of giving certain truths less than their due by overstressing others. While he cannot damage the actual substance of faith, a preacher's undue emphasis may lead such a person into errors which, transmitted in his teaching, can have the most disastrous and far-reaching consequences.

The following pages set out to prove that in recent years the accent certainly has shifted in the sphere of moral instruction. Nowadays morality is regarded almost exclusively as a question relating to sexual behavior. In modern language, the words "moral" and "chaste," "immoral" and "unchaste" are used indiscriminately. By giving sexual morals priority in the ethical sphere, all other moral issues are forced into the background. There are theologians of all denominations who honestly believe that this truly represents Christian teaching and seem quite to have forgotten that Christ Himself, without detracting in the least from chastity, summed up His whole mission by proclaiming another virtue to be the greatest of all—and that virtue was LOVE.

NOTES

1. The author goes into this more thoroughly in his *Spannungen und Harmonie* (Kevelaer, 1941), chapters II and III.
2. See Stephanus Hilpisch, O.S.B., *Geschichte des Benediktinischen mönchtums* (Freiburg im Breisgau, 1929), p. 66.
3. *Cautio criminalis,* dub. 16, 5; 24, 1; 34, 3.
4. *Zucht und Mass* (Leipzig, 1939), p. 49.
5. *Ibid.,* p. 50.

CHAPTER 2

Tracing the Historical Development of the Sexual Question

1.

WRITERS in the last few decades who have occupied themselves with the much-debated question of sex treat this question as a self-evident one, coexistent with the presence of the sexual instinct in the human being. They do not take into account that whole centuries lie behind us, in which sexual needs were equally in evidence but gave rise to no sort of problem. They confuse the personal aspect, which is conditioned by an individual's own particular reaction to his inherent sexual urge, with the fundamental question that relates the significance of this instinct to morality as a whole. Of course, the sexual instinct is an important question; and each individual has to supply the answer to it by his own behavior and his own way of life. The erotic urge not only affects every individual's personal life, but it has a vital bearing on the happiness and health of the family, on the tenacity of the race, on the welfare of the Church, and the whole of human culture, interwoven as it is with the mystery of unborn generations. On this account the sexual question will always be the concern of the combined faculties. Theologians cannot ignore it because of its bearing on the human soul; the law cannot overlook it because of its relation to legal principles; neither can the medical community leave it out of account because it is so intimately bound up with the health of the race. Poets, too, will always be drawn to it because of the high ideals and the profound conflicts it is capable of rousing. In these various respects, sex will always be a question for the human mind to tackle. But this problem is solely concerned with the exterior fulfillment of the sexual instinct and not with its inner lawfulness and the logical consequences that should be drawn from this. As far as that is concerned, there really can be no question at all; for fundamental facts about this are clear and indisputable, as even those disputants must admit who, in the main, make no particular practical efforts to be guided by those facts. A thousand adulterers can constitute no marriage problem so long as they are fully aware of breaking the law and the commandments, just as a thousand thieves create no social problem so long as the fundamental principles of right and property remain firmly rooted in the public mind as a whole.

This comparison with the origin of a social problem is very apt and throws considerable light on the process whereby the sexual question came into being. For centuries, the rights of private ownership were never called into question. It occurred to no one either to dispute them or to investigate them, although there were even in those days thieves who had no respect for private property and ignored these rights. The thief appropriated the concrete possessions of others, either because of his necessity or from sheer wickedness; but it never occurred to him to deny the fundamental rights of ownership nor had he any intention of upsetting the whole social order of his time. It was not until later, when the whole structure of private ownership had been disturbed, and property became concentrated in the hands of a few while the majority of mankind possessed little or nothing, that the question arose whether these few really had the right to all the possessions they held on to with such tenacity. The discontented at first put this question very timidly; then more joined in and, at last, the clamor became loud and insistent. It was not raised only by thieves and troublemakers; serious and honest thinkers joined in. And all at once we had a social question.

Similarly, the sexual question was not always an established fact, although the sexual instinct had always been a part of the human being. Chastity, the sacredness of the marriage bed, and marital constancy were accepted principles among healthy, virile people like the Germanic races, the Greeks, the Romans in the days before any degeneracy set in. Christianity, through revelation, planted the idea of chastity and pure conjugal fidelity still more firmly in the minds of the converted nations. Even though polygamy, female slavery, and divorce might arise here and there, introducing confused thought, they never succeeded in affecting the actual substance of chastity and marriage. "From the beginning it was not so" (Matt. 19: 8) our Lord said, replying to a question relating to divorce and thereby in a few words giving a direction on the decline of moral consciousness. The Christian principle is quite clear, and all the disrupting influences of the centuries have not succeeded in shaking it. Difficulties that have occurred from time to time in this sphere have always been of a personal nature. Even where excesses, in periods of decline, affected large multitudes, they had their origin not in any fundamental change of principle, but in the lust or weakness of individuals. It is, therefore, quite wrong to read any problem into all this because no change has taken place in the original moral pattern—not as in the case of the social problem, which actually has been brought about by a shifting of economic and social conditions. Circumstances of ownership are liable to essential change, but sex relationships do not change at all. It has sometimes happened that the outward living conditions of a whole community have altered radically in a single century—but the erotic urge, the attraction of the sexes to each other, always remained the same. Climate and race, opulence and poverty, backward culture or refinement may all help to bring about trespass in marriage, but they cannot affect the principle of marriage itself. One may meet with occasional infidelity, unchastity, and even perversity among primitive people just as among inbred, overcivilized, degenerate races; but monogamy, chastity, and loyalty may also be found just as much at home in many so-called "savage" communities as they are in the asphalt streets of our big cities.[1] The number of virtues or of vices is quite beside the point. There have been periods of great moral, or even sexual, decline without any hint of a sexual problem. And if this problem is nowadays bandied about from mouth to mouth, that is no proof of our age being the victim of any moral disaster. It is merely a challenge inviting us to study the fundamental principles of sex a little more closely in order that we may arrive at the essence of morality, chastity, and marriage. Some people look upon sex as the most sublime thing, others regard it as the most bestial; some consider it the purest, others the most unclean; some glorify it as the greatest affirmation of life, others condemn it as the denial of spirit. The solution of the problem can therefore never be found in sweeping reforms. It calls primarily for a recognition of the clash of spiritual forces out of which this Babelic confusion of opinions has grown.

If the origin of the social problem must be sought in an economic development that has gone off the rails, the clue to the sexual question can only lie in an ideological misconception which has gradually diverted sexual thought from its original healthy orientation. This is a state of affairs that calls for energetic reform.

2.

Delving into history, we always find confusion in sexual thought associated with the older races when they are approaching their decline. In its classical period, Greco-Roman culture had no sexual problem until it had passed its zenith. To the ancient Greek, chastity and marriage were very real conceptions which meant far more to the populace for the very reason that they were not publicly discussed. Historians often make the mistake of estimating the importance of a subject by the frequency with which references to it occur in literature. Yet experience shows that things only become noticeable, and thus force themselves on the attention of writers, when they grow rare and threaten to disappear from sober reality. So long as ideas are accepted as self-evident, no one bothers to discuss them. As Schiller says:

> By what can I recognize the best state? By the same that applies to the best woman, my friend—you don't talk about either!

The erotic has no place in Greek tragedy or even in comedy. Certainly, love stories existed in those days; but there was no taste in Hellas for the glamorous treatment and endless repetition of the eternal theme, the sort of thing we are served up with in our theaters, movies, popular songs, and romantic literature nowadays. As for a sexual problem, such an idea never occurred to the countless poets and philosophers of ancient Greece. Even during its period of decline, when lust and perversion spread themselves slimily over contemporary literature, vandal hands were never laid on the sacredness of sexual life; these fundamentals were protected both by religion and the laws of the state—despite Homer and the goings-on of Zeus and the other gods! It should of course be admitted that associations between men and young boys occurred and were winked at; but these unnatural practices were not officially licensed. Even in the last stages of the decline, pederasty, on paper at least, was sternly put down. The legal code of both Athens and Sparta made the crime punishable by death and loss of honor. The way in which references to this perversion are veiled, so that our philologists and historians have the greatest difficulty in detecting their meaning, proves how conscious the ancients were of the shamefulness of these pervert practices.[2]

Nor was there any marriage problem in Rome even when, according to Seneca's witty line, the women no longer counted the years by the consuls, but by the number of times they changed their husbands. With all these excesses and with all the talk about sexual freedom, public opinion held on to the healthy view that it would be better if these things did not occur. They were regrettable backslidings from the universally respected ideal. One need only read the Roman odes of Horace to confirm how earnestly he deplored the decline of manners among the people and in the state, and how clearly he foresaw the evil consequences of such debauchery.

Fecunda culpæ sæcula nuptias
Primum inquinavere et genus et domos;
Hoc fonte derivata clades
In patriam populumque fluxit

. . . . .

Ætas parentum, pejor avis, tulit
Nos nequiores, mox daturos
Progeniem vitiosiorem (Carm. 3. 6).[3]

Of course, the public conscience in those days of decline did not depend upon the priesthood to rouse it to a sense of responsibility, for the heathen temples in which the priests served were, of all places, the most unruly dens of vice in those ancient cities. In republican times it was the office of the censor to control and to judge public morals, and he usually took his duties seriously enough. With the coming of the Cæsars things changed, for they took upon themselves the title of supreme censor, which seemed to confer greater dignity and appealed to them more than that of consul, which office they delegated to men of straw. The official conscience under this new control fell asleep and soon ceased to function. The task of upholding a standard of decency then fell upon the shoulders of private individuals. It was voluntarily taken up by philosophers, usually disciples of the Stoic school, who became wandering preachers in some cases and acquired quite a following. Strange as it may seem, the writers of comedies were even more successful in keeping up the standard, for they castigated human weaknesses with the weapon of ridicule and thus succeeded in stemming the flood of filth which was gradually engulfing the empire. Paradoxically they contrived to keep the ideals of connubial fidelity and natural chastity constantly before the public. The sexual abnormalities of the day provided poets like Terence and Juvenal with rich material for their satires; and much as Ovid glories in lust, he never makes polemic capital out of it. Vice was rampant everywhere, but it never occurred to anyone to make it an excuse for debasing the ethical standard. Adultery and perversion might be multiplied a thousandfold, but not one poet or philosopher dared to justify vice or to hold it up as a pattern of pure morality.

Yet, at the time of the Roman Empire, something like a sexual problem actually did appear on the horizon, in the East. The cults of Astarte and Cybele and similar imported deities from Egypt and Syria found a hospitable welcome amid the temple prostitution of Greece and, even to some extent, in the sterner atmosphere of Rome. These cults were steadily on the increase. Here was a situation in which, for the first time, the old ideals of chastity were being completely undermined and all kinds of excesses were not merely tolerated but even advocated. Vice became almost a religious aspiration and all kinds of licentiousness were urged as a form of ecstasy. This completely reversed the former respect for the sacredness of chastity, and neither public opinion nor the law could stand up against the pernicious flood of degenerate innovations. For a long time the state tried to arrest the infiltration of sensuality. Countless edicts were issued forbidding the introduction of these pernicious Eastern cults.[4] The Emperor Tiberius had Egyptian priests crucified and their temples razed to the ground. Hadrian passed laws prohibiting the "foreigners"—that is to say, non-Greeks and non-Romans—from entering his territory. The strength of the general public's fundamentally healthy convictions may be gathered from the uproar caused when Heliogabalus' unnatural practices were condemned by the populace. It must be remembered, of course, that the young and growing community of Christians was already bringing its moral support to the aid of the tottering power of Rome in matters of public morality. The ultimate overcoming of the poison germ must be attributed entirely to the Christian elements, for both the state and the leaders of heathen society were becoming less and less capable of resisting the evil oriental influences. The very plethora of state edicts and prohibitions on the subject proves their futility. Apart from Christianity the resistance becomes weaker and weaker, especially as the later Roman emperors set their subjects a very bad example —it must be admitted that some of their predecessors did no better—and ended by giving the oriental innovations free play. The fact that the political overthrow of the Roman Empire did not—as history might lead us to expect—go hand in hand with its complete moral decay but, on the contrary, coincided with a regeneration from within which eventually enabled Rome to triumph over its own ruin is indisputably due to the Christian Church which, by its teaching and its example, overcame the devastating consequences of oriental vice. Pious Christian matrons, virtuous virgins, and untarnished marriages established an ideal of righteous living which benighted heathen observers could not resist.

This struggle, which ran its course in the third, fourth and fifth centuries, was all the more obstinate because Hellenic philosophy about this time formed an alliance with perverse religious mysticism. Plato's teaching about the body as "the prison of the soul" [5] was developed with fateful consequences by the Neoplatonists who chose to interpret the Platonic concept as a feud between soul and body. The consequent distrust of anything physical or material took the form, in Neoplatonism, of a rigid rigorism which not only forbade indulgence in meat and wine but also prohibited sexual intercourse even within the bonds of marriage. The stand the Neoplatonists took was that these were all incompatible with a truly spiritual life since they kept the soul fettered to its prison, the body, and materialism, and were therefore sinful. Despite its many admirable intentions, the primary conditions of Neoplatonism drew it more and more within the orbit of oriental Dualism which explained the world as being the creation of the devil and therefore wholly evil in substance. These two schools of thought eventually merged in Manicheism, the heresy which, in the third and fourth centuries, became such a menace not only to Christianity but to all natural, moral concepts. The more radical an idea, the more readily it appeals to people who are always attracted to popular movements and give them no deep thought. It is not surprising that, in an age of widespread degeneracy and licentiousness, the recoil provided fertile soil for teachings of such seeming idealism, advocating, as they did, the highest moral integrity and the most noble spiritual aims while disdaining materialism with the utmost contempt. Catholic teaching of the divinely ordained harmony between spirit and body was condemned by these fanatics who looked upon it as a weak half measure, a spineless concession to human frailty. That was why the Manichean gnostics called the Catholics "psychics" and gave themselves the superior name of "pneumatics" or "the spiritual." They believed themselves, of course, to be immeasurably better than the low-down "hyloists" or materialists who were unrepentant heathens, completely given over to the indulgence of the senses. How spellbinding these high-flown ideas must have been to young people whose own ideals were lofty is shown by the fact that even a serious thinker like St. Augustine was blinded by them for a time, during his student days at Carthage. Only as he reached maturity was he able to recognize the cloven hoof in this teaching, the unhealthy effects of severing soul from body and setting them against each other antagonistically. The consequence, on the one hand, was an exaggerated so-called "spiritualization" that looked with contempt on the body and its legitimate needs, requiring its followers to submit to unnatural and impossible restrictions; and on the other hand an equally uninhibited materialism, a complete surrender to sensual lust, in which the teaching saw no fault since the cult considered itself outside the normal laws of behavior and subject to a superior order of morality. *Les extrêmes se touchent.* For it follows that if soul and body are mutually antagonistic opposites, they can in noway influence each other. Therefore, the most unclean actions on the part of a "spiritual" cannot be sinful because the spiritual and the physical belong to different worlds, and therefore a besmirching of the spirit through the body is impossible. The soul is so immeasurably higher than the body that it is quite independent of it and cannot possibly be touched by anything the body may do. And this provides a formula for indulging in the greatest licentiousness without any loss of piety or self-esteem. With such a philosophy, one man could renounce the world and another could be an unabashed libertine; not infrequently the two found themselves cheerfully united in one and the same person—idealistic teaching and hedonic practice.

Thus arose that remarkable compound of prudery and brutality, of strained ecstasy and base self-indulgence, of fine phrasemaking and shameless cant which, with all its cheapness, had the effrontery to pose as righteousness, flaunting a mantle of superior morality.

In this sultry atmosphere, full of hypocritical distortion, the sexual problem was born—and the same atmosphere has surrounded it ever since. The whole gnosis of the time is conditioned by these mutual contradictions. While the Nicolaites (Apoc. 2: 6-14) preached female communism, the Platonists like Carpocrates, Epiphanes, etc., repulsed the adherents of Marcian; and the Encratites, followers of Tatian, forbade wine drinking, flesh eating and marriage as being all equally sinful in their view. Manicheism, also called the Persian Gnosis, embraced within itself all the opposing elements and was largely responsible for spreading this poisonous and overstrained ethical concept, which had previously been confined to philosophical circles where it was comparatively harmless, to the far wider circle of the ordinary public.

Manicheism was the father of the sexual question. Whenever and wherever Manichean ideas have cropped up—in antiquity, in the Middle Ages, or in modern times—they have attacked simple, clear thinking on the subjects of chastity and morality, bending and distorting the natural moral laws established from the beginnings of time and confirmed by the teaching of revelation, The question turns into a problem when we reflect that it is only part—though perhaps the most important part—of a still wider question, namely, that of the relationship of a Christian to the world around him. What is his position in regard to worldly affairs, to ownership and property, to art and science, to economics and to the state, to marriage and social intercourse, to dancing, music, the theater, alcohol, and so on?

The Catholic Church waged war on Manicheism in ancient times and triumphed over it. This heresy was, for a time, the Church's greatest rival in wrestling for the oriental soul. Had Manichean ideas gained the mastery, Eastern thought would have penetrated into our midst and the history of Western culture might forever have remained unwritten.

The struggle was especially violent and the danger insidious when Gnostic-Manichean thought-forms repeatedly tried to gain a foothold in ecclesiastical circles. Apart from its pretensions to a higher moral tone, Manicheism forced breaches in our defenses through the very fact that so many of its claims bore a close resemblance to Christian principles. Superficial popular thinking readily accepts errors when they cloak themselves in a mantle of idealism. Loyal Catholics were easily impressed by the Manichean claims to higher morality and by the airs they gave themselves about suppressing physical instincts and leading a wholly spiritual life. The abstinence on which the Manichean insisted was also acceptable to Christians, though from totally different motives. It is not difficult to understand how Christians were tempted to join in the disdain of all things physical, not to be behindhand in this contest to decide who was more strictly moral. St. Paul had to contend with both extremes which were particularly in evidence in Corinth, the great harbor city where East and West met in commerce which went hand in hand with an exchange on an intellectual level regarding questions of religion and ethics. While on the one hand faced with unbridled license, which regarded the satisfaction of the sexual appetite to be as natural and essential as eating and drinking and considered it morally negligible (I Cor. 6:13), St. Paul also had to take cognizance of the overstrained moral sensitiveness of many Christians who believed all sexual instincts to be unclean and sinful, thereby casting a slur even on marriage itself. The swing of the pendulum from heathen licentiousness made Christians particularly receptive to such ideas in the period immediately following the decline. Rigorous reaction, for instance, to the notion of second marriage and a penitential strictness that meted out the most severe penances to moral offenders, seemed to many extremists in the Christian community more laudable than the milder middle way, which they regarded as a weak yielding to laxity. The most glaring example of this stern code was the African Tertullian whose zeal for the Church eventually drove him out of the Church because he could not tolerate the so-called "laxity" of Pope Callistus. Yet this same "laxity" on the part of the pope was nothing more than the papal permission for true penitents to be received back into the Church. The great Origen was also too loyal a disciple of Plato not to be influenced by the latter's teaching in regard to the soul. He, too, leaned to the Neoplatonic view which casts contempt on the body, a tendency which he passed on to many of his disciples—and not only in theory. His interpretation of the passage in Matt. 19:12 caused him to go so far as to emasculate himself, an act for which he was severely reprimanded by his bishop. This case is specific proof of the unfaltering energy with which the official Church has always countered Manichean and similar ideas which were never even remotely tolerated by the Church itself, although some of its individual members, not even excluding men of intelligence and the highest integrity, might at times be carried away by them. Since these were vulnerable, who could blame the unthinking masses for being even more dazzled by such deceptive influences? The most appealing work in praise of virginity to be written in ancient Christian times, the *Banquet* by Methodius of Olympus, is not entirely free from certain doubtful exaggerations and therefore met with some criticism, even in his own day. On the other hand, Cyprian, Ambrose, and even Jerome, with all their enthusiasm for virginity, do not forget to underline the sanctity of marriage, thus clearly demonstrating the difference between Manichean contempt of the married state and the Catholic ideal of celibacy.

Danger from the intrusion of unhealthy tendencies was greatest in the Eastern monastic systems, especially as the Christian and Manichean forms of asceticism, outwardly at least, had much in common. Celibacy and fasting, self-denial of comforts and permitted indulgences can be undertaken from very different motives. The most varied and often quite contradictory movements have, at different times, demanded temperance and abstinence from their followers. To cite an almost frivolous example, one need only mention the sacrifices fashion and beauty culture impose upon their feminine devotees. A stern confessor would scarcely dare to condemn his penitents to similar self-denial by way of penance. The Stoics advocated self-discipline and abstinence to show their contempt of the world; and the Epicureans submitted to the same discipline merely to prolong their moments of enjoyment. The Manicheans' asceticism was based on their hatred of the world, just as the Indian fakir of today still practices the most extraordinary forms of self-torture out of a yearning for Nirvana. But the Christian's self-denial was not adopted for its own sake; it was undertaken for the love of God and for one's neighbor. Without this love, every sacrifice—even martyrdom and the relinquishment of all one's possessions—is "as sounding brass or a tinkling cymbal" (I Cor. 13:1). So, even though other systems, both natural and heathen, may adopt forms of self-denial very similar to our own, Christian asceticism will always differ from them essentially and radically because it springs from within. Occasionally in the West —far more often in the Orient—one comes across professional monastic forms of asceticism which seem to spring more from Dualism than from Christian models. In such matters as clothing and food, in their complete abstention from every kind of civilized refinement and comfort, even down to such details as cleanliness and bathing as well as in the studied practice of every variety of self-torture, some of these systems present a very distorted picture of the virtue of self-denial, one which serves to link asceticism in general and Catholic celibacy in particular with Manichean principles. Moreover, such misrepresentations were never the rule, but always the exception. The Church never encouraged or recommended them. And when they are mentioned from time to time in lives of the saints, the commentary *admirandum, sed non imitandum* rarely fails to make its appearance. In other words, while these forms of self-denial show a heroism which calls for respect, there is no reason to imitate them. And ruthless though they were in practicing penance upon their own persons, the charge of being self-centered and indifferent to the call of culture could hardly be leveled at those ascetic early hermit-monks who literally caused the desert to blossom by their unremitting labors. A very intense intellectual life flourished among the ascetics of the Nile; men like Athanasius, Basil, and Chrysostom gained their monastic education from the hermits of Egypt and Syria. Never, in the writings of these monks or of those who wrote about them, do we find a single line condemning marriage or debasing womankind; never a curse against men of wealth and property. "Property is not a thing that should be thrown away, or escaped from, as if it were something evil" writes the organizer of the oriental monastic system, Basil the Great.[6] "In every station of life there are souls pleasing to God, therefore it is certain that a man's calling, or the clothes he wears, are not the things God looks at, but the honesty and the love in his soul." Thus spoke Paphnutius, one of the most important of the Anchorites.[7] Bishop Keppler, in a long chapter of his delightful book *More Joy,* gives a vivid picture of the refined and truly spiritual culture, the devout yet happy attitude toward life that existed among these early fathers in the wilderness.

As far as the West is concerned, the great originator of the Western monastic system, St. Benedict, was an unrelenting opponent of ascetic excesses and his rule rejects them completely. The essential difference between the Western and the Eastern concept of monasticism lies in the fact that St. Benedict departed from earlier custom and refused to regard penitence and the castigation of the flesh as a monk's primary duty. Anthony or Pachomius might insist on the utmost limitation of life's requirements—might content themselves with one meal per day, consisting of roots and herbs; upon complete abstinence from wine, the shortest possible periods of sleep and rough, even dirty, clothing; even the Irish monk Columban might wander over the countryside with his disciples as living examples of asceticism on a more or less Eastern pattern.[8] But St. Benedict did away with all this, for he did not wish it to appear that good works were made better in proportion to the amount of pain and discomfort they caused to the doer. He ruled that two kinds of food should appear on the refectory table twice daily, and that a moderate amount of wine might be taken by those who were sick or engaged in heavy, laborious work. A monk, he ruled, must respect personal hygiene and live in cleanliness and order; he should bathe frequently, and wear better and more carefully groomed clothing on Sundays and when on a journey than when going about his ordinary tasks. He should take the necessary amount of sleep in order to rise refreshed and be able to praise God with a clear brain. The important factor of St. Benedict's rule of education for his monks is his insistence that body and spirit should be in harmony. His aim is *honestas morum*, but not in the sense of an outward education in good behavior, as the *honnête homme* of the Age of Enlightenment envisaged it. His ideal was the attainment of the highest possible perfection *from within*, through the simultaneous cooperation of spirit, soul, and body. He did not seek to attain this end by total abstinence but by moderation; not in ignoring things as they were but in using them for the highest possible good. A monk should joyfully and thankfully accept the good that God gives; but he should with the same joy be ready to relinquish, when God's will or charity toward his neighbor requires it—that was St. Benedict's idea. To pile up feats of self-denial and asceticism is not the most important thing; one should keep to the happy medium—*discretio;* not do without necessities for the sake of demonstrating one's will power, but rise above them in such a way that things which seem desirable can be enjoyed or given up as principle or the love of God requires. Through this wise rule, the Order of St. Benedict opened up cultural possibilities as neither Eastern nor Western asceticism had ever done before. St. Benedict, not St. Columban, became the pioneer of Western culture, and we have him and his followers to thank, not only for many blessings of the Christian religion, but also for encouragement of the arts and education, for the preservation of ancient writings, for the clearing of forests and for civilizing countless backward races; for introducing the use of medicinal herbs and even for many of the "trimmings" of life, such as the select beers and fine liqueurs which to this day bear the names of Benedictine monasteries. Even though there may be some who mock at this, it still belongs to the rounded out and pleasing picture of mankind in the midst of an ever developing, spiritually refined, cultural civilization, one which cannot justly be attributed to pure self-indulgence and materialism. The Benedictine is the spiritual reverse of the Puritan. Just because its whole ideal of perfection was based on the harmony of the world with the supernatural realm, the Benedictine Order was much exposed to worldly corruption; and human frailty, the leaden weight concealed in all idealism, did occasionally turn this danger into a reality. It is fascinating to notice how, in the recoil from such disloyalty to the original idea, the oriental ideal of ascetic retirement from the world crops up again and again. Thus, many a later reformer of the Order, in the belief that he was restoring St. Benedict's original idea, has misjudged all that was finest and most profound in his achievement and, with a heavy hand, has inserted ascetic ideals of the East to replace the more precious portions that have fallen away.[9] St. Benedict's ideal of perfection, which is based on the thoughts of St. Augustine, does not confine itself to the monastic order alone; it is the ideal of every Christian. No one has more clearly traced the harmony between soul and body, between nature and the supernatural, than St. Benedict, and related it even to the minutest detail of daily life. There was no rift between body and spirit, between the natural world and the supernatural—and therefore no sexual question—so long as the Western world allowed itself to be guided by this harmony. St. Benedict's rule was a logical follow-through of the Church's teaching which always kept to the exact middle of the road and rejected overstrained spiritualization just as uncompromisingly as it rejected materialism. Contemporaneously with the founding of the Benedictine Order, Manicheism disappears from the historic scene in Europe. At the Synod of Braga in 561, the last remnants of it, the teachings of Priscillian, were ejected from the Church.[10] From this time on, we see the young Germanic races taking more and more to Christianity, and Benedictine monks as the advance guard who converted them. The cultural life of the Western world follows in the wake of the monastic teachers and, for centuries, the sexual question vanishes completely from spiritual life. The fundamental principles of chaste morality and connubial fidelity, so deeply rooted in the Germanic race, are in essential accord with the Christian way of thinking. Tacitus' description of the race and its moral customs in ancient times is fully endorsed by St. Augustine and Salvian at the time of the Migration of Nations. The decline of the East Goths and the Vandals can be traced largely to their contact with the degenerate populace of the ancient world, which contributed no less than the softening effect of the unaccustomed southern climate to the undermining of their moral, as well as their physical, resistance. Nor was it advantageous to the West Goths and the Franks that, in Merovingian times, a certain relaxation of their ancient tribal morality set in, and there were some hard struggles before the sense of responsibility inherent in the Christian faith had thoroughly established itself. There were many false steps in the sexual realm, and the Church had many battles to fight; but all these difficulties, despite their abundance, were of a personal nature. They rose from passion, or tyranny, or lust for power, but were never caused by a collapsing ideology.

It must be obvious to anyone who enters thoroughly into the spirit of the Middle Ages, by studying the art, the literature, the folk customs, and the prayers of the period, that it knew no "sexual question." The complete lack of inhibition, the naïveté, and the genuine matter-of-factness with which our forefathers took the body and its needs for granted has become quite foreign to modern man and strikes him as being an attitude so crude that it sometimes antagonizes him. Sex was simply an integral part of the whole man, no more and no less. It had its rights and its confines. Taken for granted as a thing one did not discuss or write compendiums about, it was, in essence, protected by the law and still more by sacred tradition. And that was how not a breath of impurity attached to it, not the slightest hint of its being a thing that should preferably not exist. A saintly woman like St. Hildegard could without embarrassment offer her medical knowledge on sexual organs—they were as natural as any other part of the human make-up requiring a doctor's help. Even before her time, the poetess-nun Hroswitha had incorporated in her dramas some quite gripping scenes, in which the alluring process of falling in love was depicted as glamorously as possible in order, as she contended, "to emphasize the honor due to the superior claims of divine grace." [11] Mystics like Eckhart and Suso make comparisons between heavenly love and sexual love as a matter of course. The art of the time treated with honest realism intimate details which a more sensitive later age considered offensive, and rigorously rejected. In this connection it is only necessary to recall the numerous representations of the Circumcision and of aspects of childbearing, as, for instance, in the magnificent picture recording the life of our Lady in the Richartz-Wallraf Museum in Cologne. Even works depicting the Infant Jesus in His Mother's womb, and examples like that moving representation of the Annunciation, one of the most beautiful oil paintings of the Cologne School now to be found in the Gallery of Utrecht, were not uncommon and show how little the intimacy of sex was a source of embarrassment to the medieval mind. The celebrated miraculous picture of the Madonna at the popular pilgrimage resort of Bogenberg near Straubing was a similar representation. It had a tiny door which, when opened, revealed the Infant Jesus in the very womb of the Holy Mother. It is quite obvious that such works as these were not just "stunts" carried out by painters to increase their notoriety. The multitude of this class of paintings proves that. Hidden away in countless old churches are similar studies no longer publicly hung, and the deep religious sincerity that clearly emanates from them is the best possible evidence that their creators were not conscious of any breach of common decency in painting such subjects. The often misused words of the Apostle, "All things are clean to the clean" (Tit. 1:15), genuinely do apply here. In times when the consciousness of moral values is untroubled by doubts, there is no need for prudish anxiety. It would be far more to the point if, in the face of such complete absence of self-consciousness, we asked ourselves what has happened to our own moral attitude, since we now take exception to things which our ancestors held sacred.

We get the same impression from the folk customs of the Middle Ages, especially those that have any connection with betrothal, marriage, and the blessing of children. The bridal bed received the priest's solemn blessing, and many pictures show that when this blessing took place the young couple immediately made use of it. The young couple on their wedding day (invariably called "consummation") were not only escorted to Church and to the banquet that followed, but to the very bridal chamber by their friends and relations. The scene in Wagner's *Lohengrin* which dramatizes this is completely authentic. Certainly this practice sometimes led to abuses, which the preachers of the time wholeheartedly condemned. But it was the abuse, not the custom itself, that gave cause for objection.[12] Then again, bathing houses were perhaps more commonly in use during the Middle Ages than at any other time. Even in the most humble circles it was customary to bathe on the eve of Sundays and all feast days (of which there were a multitude). There were many public bathing houses; Vienna alone had twenty-nine in the fourteenth century; in Breslau there were twelve and in Frankfort-on-the-Main, fifteen.[13] Pious benefactors (the so-called "soul-bathers") saw to it that even the poorest had the necessary facilities for practicing bodily cleanliness—and it was customary to call the tip which one gave to a workman for any personal service his "bath money," not his "drink money." About the time of the Crusades, communal bathing places used by both sexes indiscriminately began to take the place of the older establishments in which men and women were strictly segregated; and this not unnaturally gave rise to disorderly conduct against which the preachers of the time were compelled to make loud protest. It would be quite false to describe the sexual behavior of that period as essentially decorous. "It is difficult to determine whether public morality in the Middle Ages was of a higher or a lower standard than at any other time. But one fact emerges which distinguishes it sharply from the attitude of both the antique and of the modern world. The medieval sinner was as conscious of his trespass as he was of the necessity of doing penance for it. The swing of the pendulum was already taking in a wider sweep between the extremes of good and evil. Sexual matters were in the main discussed pretty freely, as a glance at the legal proceeding of the age will clearly show. Many hoaxes and naïve practical jokes originated in these times—they seem to us very coarse and crude, but we cannot dispute the fact that the whole tone of behavior was more honest than that of our own epoch, which hides behind locked doors everything that was then trotted out quite openly. It is precisely this open and uninhibited behavior that proves there was no 'sexual question' in those times" (R. Allers).

But perhaps the most convincing proof of all lies in the fact that the Middle Ages produced no literature whatsoever on the subject. The question, "How shall I explain to my child?" which so oppresses many modern parents simply did not exist in those days. Among all the countless pamphlets dealing with religious themes, which circulated freely among the general public after the invention of the "Black Art," we cannot find one that occupies itself with this burning question even in the most remote way.[14] As the child grew up, he automatically made his own discoveries about the mysteries of the unborn without ever standing in need of any special explanations. Pictures, prayers, and old customs provided the necessary impressions which enabled the child to absorb the necessary information without being conscious of anything out-of-the-ordinary, much less impure, being connected with it. The fact that he became accustomed to seeing the origin of human life in a religious setting from the very start gave that knowledge an aura of sacredness, quite free from the pomp of "enlightenment" in its idealized, pedagogic sense. Our Catholic past knew how to rate the intimate, lofty, God-ordained relationship of marriage partners, the tender relationship between mother and child, far more highly than the modern age which is so inordinately proud of its superior moral attitude.

3.

How, then, did the sexual problem, which nowadays undoubtedly exists, really originate?

Slight beginnings of conditions favorable to its development had always existed, not, as in later periods, in the leanings of pastoral theology, but in the doctrinal trend, strongly colored, as it was, by monastic asceticism. Early scholastic thought was too closely directed towards Platonic philosophy for its spiritual tendencies not to have resulted in a disdainful attitude toward the senses. Thus the ground was well prepared and, at any moment, germs hatched in the solitude of monastic cells—with the best of intentions—could have spread a poison virus and once again infected the world with that very sexual problem against which the ancient Church had waged such valiant and, fortunately, successful warfare.

But the roots of the sexual problem lie deepest in Nominalism which ever since the thirteenth century has been more and more strikingly recurrent in the intellectual life of the Western world. According to this concept, reality exists only in individual things. This leads to the splitting up of everything that exists into "elements" and further units. The tendency toward "dividing into parts," from the time of the Renaissance and the Reformation right down to the materialistic era, has been becoming more and more noticeable. The unity of God and His world, of nature and the supernatural, which was the sheet anchor of medieval man's philosophy, has been exploded into innumerable parts and harmony has vanished in the process. Just as, in the ancient world, related religious questions attached themselves to Neoplatonic philosophy, the Nominalistic thought processes of modern times began to touch upon some of the more extreme religious ideas. On every hand Manicheism raised its head again, under different guises. Natural, clear thinking became confused concerning the relation of nature to the supernatural, man to the world; and this upset the well-ordered attitude toward sex and the senses as a whole, bringing down with it the whole complex structure of morality. A. M. Weiss has demonstrated in a most convincing way the stages by which the split between the world and the supernatural, between body and soul, grew out of Nominalism; and how this division, spread through the teachings of the Reformation, found more and more acceptance in the intellectual world until the road was thoroughly cleared for Manicheism and other Oriental concepts.[15] Individual currents of Manicheism had of course already found entry before this, partly traceable to the Crusades, partly to the trade connections that linked up the East, via the Balkans, with Lombardy and the merchant cities. They had brought sects like the Albigensians, Bogomiles, and so on into being; [16] but, thanks to energetic action on the part of the ecclesiastical and state authorities, as well as to the as yet unshaken faith of the vast majority, these heresies were confined to comparatively limited areas. All the same, they were never entirely wiped out, but kept cropping up again, in one form or another, particularly in religious circles—the Fraticelli of southern Italy, and the Beguines [17] of the Lowlands are apt examples. The confusion which followed the Reformation brought these various religious undercurrents to the surface and secured them wider publicity. The radical tendency in religion and philosophy was their connecting link. A literary work prepared for the Landgrave Philip of Hesse shows how at that time attempts were being made to undermine the time-honored attitude toward morality.[18] What the court theologians have to say against unity in marriage, to please their patron, smacks more of Byzantium than of inner conviction. But the fact that impious hands were laid on something which the mass of the public held sacred shows that here we have the very beginnings of a problem in the making. Luther's teaching, that the whole nature of man was ruined by original sin,[19] that this sin consists essentially of desire [20] and that "marriage is a worldly act, just like eating, drinking and sleeping," [21] forecasts the direction and further development of what eventually became the sexual question. The more these teachings became common property, the more the established principles of the sacramental quality, the unity, and the indissolubility of marriage were called into question—and with them vanished all the old values of chastity and virginity within the framework of morality. It was really more a fortunate coincidence than a logical development that the ultimate, most radical consequences of this teaching did not immediately set in and that precisely in Lutheran circles the sanctity of family life was particularly stressed and fostered. Luther himself was anything but a Manichean; his whole life-loving nature rejected this somber philosophy. It almost seems as if his belligerent way of putting over ideas, which was at times quite a bit overdone, was chosen chiefly to annoy his adversaries, his own actions proved that even he did not take them too seriously! Proof of this lies not only in the firm stand he took against the proceedings of men like Karlstadt, but still more in his energetic repudiation of his own disciple, Flacius Illyricus, in whose teachings Manicheism openly reappears. However, the stone had started rolling and nothing could stop it. Inevitably there were others, more radical and consistent in their thought than the first reformer, who ruthlessly drew from his premises the conclusions to which they logically led. As the evangelical theologian, K. Auer,[22] writes: "The Reformation attitude to the reality of sin, which in Luther is always tied up with the sublime idea of redemption (pecca fortiter!), has been flattened underfoot. One wallowed in the gloomy blackening of unregenerate man, who was more worthless than a stone or a tree-stump." All the same, Luther's milder attitude in practice helped to insure a certain restraint in later German Protestantism, and these effectively barred the way to Manichean ideas.

Calvinism, on the other hand, proved itself in this respect, and in many other questions, more consistent and therefore more radical. Puritanism, with its gloomy ethics, was one of the products of its very first struggles and illustrates all the ruggedness of Calvinistic thought. The Manicheism of ancient times appears again in its judgment of the world and worldly affairs as a whole. The world being evil through and through, the Christian cannot do better than isolate himself from it as much as possible, if he wishes to approach perfection. This antagonistic attitude to nature and to all the pleasures of the senses turned the Puritans into enemies of art and learning, an enmity which expressed itself in the breaking up of churches, destruction of pictures and statues and other works of art. They were fanatic total abstainers, and condemned all forms of sensual pleasure. Calvin's own model state, in Geneva, the reformed *Civitas Dei*, incorporated his principles. It subordinated all public and private life to his own strict moral censorship, did away with all natural joy, and even forbade children to laugh on the streets. This ascetic way of life has remained a part of Calvinism in its essential principles right down to the present day. It expresses itself in general behavior, in the extreme sobriety of its religigous observances, and even in the recommendations laid down for dress and the arrangement of the hair. M. Weber[23] and E. Troeltsch[24] even speak of an "ascetic aspect" in the business transactions of the Calvinists, a spirit from which modern capitalism has sprung. After many original setbacks, Puritanism succeeded in gaining an influential position in reformed theology toward the end of the sixteenth century.[25] In Holland, England, and America it acquired a greater following than the more moderate Lutheran form. It made a particularly strong impression on the English and American clergy. In England, it colored the whole political picture for a time; and, in America, it was able to continue its development without hindrance because the restrictions which had kept it under control in the English motherland were not in existence there.

Puritanism is the cradle and the vehicle of the sexual question of modern times. In England, it cut adrift at an early period from the established church and split up into several minor sects. Their task is to establish the Kingdom of God and, like the Montanists of old, they mean by this community only the elect—those who are holy and utterly pure. Of course, as fanatical Protestants, they could not adopt monastic asceticism; but the orthodox practiced abstinence from meat and alcohol and every refinement of life just as rigidly as the anchorites of olden times; and, instead of living in the Egyptian wilderness, the Pilgrim Fathers migrated to the primeval forests of New England, there to enjoy full "liberty of conscience" without any interference from the state. The history of the state of Massachusetts proves that the steady increase of emigration, starting with the voyage of the *Mayflower* in 1620, was not merely a movement stimulated by commerce and politics, but was at least equally determined by religious zeal.

There is no question of the sincerity of these ascetics. Theirs was the honest but unenlightened religious enthusiasm which resulted in such a remarkable outcrop of sects during the sixteenth and seventeenth centuries. But inevitably this overstrained enthusiasm led in the end to the same contradictions which gave the Gnosticism of olden times its sinister character. On the one hand, the moral approach led to a grim ruthlessness which tyrannized over public life and forced everyone to conform to the views of the dominant sect. On the other hand, the need of compromise with the sinful world became inescapable, as soon as the first flush of enthusiasm had worn off. The natural instinct for joy and companionship was driven underground. And in addition, the sexual instinct, which could not be denied, was outwardly repudiated as being beneath contempt but secretly often led to practices which were quite out of keeping with genuine morality. Thus arose that compelling sense of shame which robbed people of the power to distinguish between natural instincts and depravity—a state of mind that is always on edge, because it confuses the two different issues; an oversensitive state in which natural shame becomes unnatural, a state that eventually leads to the hypocritical behavior we call prudery. By this we mean an unbending moral attitude which regards everything sexual as impure and, therefore, seeks to ignore it—an inflated sense of shame behind which, by the law of extremes, private lust may quite frequently lurk. It is noteworthy that, in past times, there can have been no conception of this mixture of outward primness and insincerity, for the world had not even thought of a name for it. The word "prudery" originally had quite a friendly ring; it meant understandability, denoting that a thing was worthy of being honored. Not until the seventeenth century did the word's present meaning establish itself, first in England, then in France. Germany, which even to this day does not possess [26] a comparable expression of its own, adopted it as late as the eighteenth century.[27] About the same time, England invented the similar but still more expressive word "cant" which, unlike "prudery," is still so typically Anglo-Saxon that no one can disguise the fact that it originated in the very nature of the English religious sects. The word comes from the Latin *cantus*, and originally denoted the singsong of affected piety which was so typical at gatherings of pietistic devotees. It was the kind of thing, for instance, that Fontane had in mind when he coined the famous sarcasm: One says God and means Gold; one speaks of Humanity and means Calico. Authors like Carlyle, Dickens, and Ruskin; painters like Hogarth and Rowlandson were tireless in heaping on it their scorn and ridicule.[28] But an attitude rooted in religious and political views which have become quite profitable is not so easily put to rout by artists and literary men.

Nowhere is this split mental attitude more clearly illustrated than in the interpretation of the Sixth Commandment. With fine speeches anything could be justified, except just one thing—a sexual scandal. In this respect, society, which had a euphemistic word for almost every crime, was absolutely immovable. Sexual irregularities were, of course, winked at—provided they hid themselves decently behind closed doors. But anyone who braved publicity by offending openly, found society's "iron curtain" firmly down, and the largest stones were invariably cast by those who were hiding similar offenses in their own lives with all the circumspection which "decency" demanded. A fallen woman was universally shunned—the law condemned her to the whipping post and the workhouse; and no matter how many tears of repentance she might shed, they could not purchase her a passport back into the ranks of the respectable. Only one sin remained, the unpardonable sin of "immorality," which was simply boiled down to sexual offense—and even that was only a sin if the sinner was found out. The whole of religion became a matter of morality, and the whole of morality was concentrated in the Sixth Commandment, to the exclusion or at least neglect of all the other nine. And in the history of language, this also gives us the clue as to why, about this time, the expressions "moral" and "chaste" began to take on identical meanings.

One of the best-known authorities on Puritanism, W. Dibelius, weighing up the disadvantages and advantages which it has passed on to other sects, believes its strict attitude towards morality—as opposed to the cruder and freer attitude of former times—to be the greatest benefit Puritanism has bestowed. G. K. Chesterton is of the opposite opinion. Puritanism, he maintains, murdered Merry Old England by its exaggerated strictness. It deprived the people of all humor and all inborn joy. He mourns the hearty laughter that once echoed through baronial halls and taverns, even slyly creeping at times into the dry theological disputations our medieval forefathers loved—this happy laughter, Chesterton maintains, the Puritans did their best to silence and, for a time, they succeeded in doing so; indeed, since then, it has never been quite so spontaneous or universal. This was one of the main causes of turning Chesterton's inclinations toward Catholicism, to which in the end he was converted. He goes even further in probing the matter, for he makes the observation that the people in countries that remained loyal to the old faith, far from justifying the reproach of asceticism and gloomy renunciation of the world, exhibit far more natural happiness and an uninhibited joy of living which is seldom found among those whose piety and morality were "reformed" by the Reformation. "Catholic doctrine and discipline may be walls; but they are the walls of a playground. . . . We might fancy some children playing on the flat grassy top of some tall island in the sea. So long as there was a wall round the cliff's edge they could fling themselves into every frantic game and make the place the noisiest of nurseries. But the walls were knocked down, leaving the naked peril of the precipice. They did not fall over; but when their friends returned to them they were all huddled in terror in the centre of the island; and their song had ceased." [29] Which of the two evaluations is the correct one will always depend on the religious standpoint from which they are respectively viewed. Two indisputable facts, however, stand out. The first is that the puritanical spirit, once it had established itself in private life and in public affairs, had an exceedingly far-reaching influence, and not infrequently a narrowing one. Both in England and in the United States, public opinion exercised a censorship which exceeded even the law in its severity. It controlled the people's pleasures, their drama, their literature and even, for a considerable time, held up scientific progress in the important sphere of sexual study. The second fact that emerges is the drastic narrowing down of the concept of morality which, from the time of the Puritans onward, becomes almost exclusively a matter of sex and of alcoholism. America's Prohibition, as we all know, was a movement sponsored almost entirely by puritanical interests. It would, of course, be quite wrong to condemn the whole system indiscriminately. The intentions of the puritanical sects aimed high, and their stern, forbidding faces often hid many sterling virtues—among them unswerving resolution, sobriety, industry, and great love of family with all its attendant domestic attributes. But one cannot escape the conclusion that their superior moral tone—(an expression the Manicheans of early Christian times were incidentally also fond of applying to themselves)—which brought these virtues in its train, even when it was genuine, could only be purchased at the cost of even greater moral values, and that must be regarded as altogether too high a price to pay.

In assessing the lowering of moral values that characterizes modern thought and has its roots in the Manichean influence which confuses judgment in matters of right and wrong, it is also a mistake to lay the whole blame at the door of Puritanism. Certainly the particular characteristics of this outlook found the climate of England and America most congenial to their development; but that may have been due to the liberal constitutions of these nations, which gave them a great measure of freedom. It is also true that, in religious matters, there was a strong link between England and the Continent, and the connection was particularly close with Germany. Here, Protestantism had been noticeably colored by Calvinism from the start, so that even in its land of origin the milder teaching of Luther soon found itself involved in a whirlpool of schism, the more drastic Geneva reformer forcing the Lutherans into an attitude of defense. But Puritanism went beyond all other tendencies in its belligerent fanaticism. So far as Germany was concerned, the consequences were delayed by the political power of petty princes. Jealous of their own right to control the consciences of their subjects, they took care not to let fanatical democrats coolly snatch their religious authority from their grasp. Contrasts between free thinking and outward form were also less obvious in Germany because the little absolutists who ruled at the minor courts of Central Europe felt themselves in no way obliged to use metaphorical fig leaves or conceal their mimicry of the regal goings on at Versailles, which they all regarded as being rather smart and fashionable. Still, if the spread of puritanical ideas in Germany was retarded, the seeds had been sown there as elsewhere and eventually they came to fruition. The epidemic broke out in a rash of sects that followed all the familiar footprints of Puritanism, and the little states of Germany were torn by many a sharp conflict between the leaders of these sects and the princely heads of the established religion. The movement was as much furthered by the hairsplitting "letter of the law" theology of Luther as by the genuine desire of many pious Protestants for a free state of worship, one not controlled by the self-seeking views of an absolute sovereign. Here, too, the tendency was toward a complete and energetic rejection of all dogma, and a narrowing down of the religious concept until it covered only a strict morality or, at most, the exaggerated, overstrained mysticism of Pietism. Valuable as the achievements of an earnest soul like Angelus Silesius, or Francke of Halle, who did so much to make charity a living virtue, might be, these pietistic groups were nevertheless mainly distinguished by their boundless sentimentality and their overemphatic stand on certain moral aspects. And the other extreme was also to be met. In the hymnbook of the Moravian-Herrnhuter sect, we come across verses which, by their frequent double meanings and their undercurrent of lust, read like caricatures when compared with the simplicity and complete lack of self-consciousness of the early German mystics. We read of a sect in Frankfurt, the members of which practiced mixed bathing, stark naked, singing the while "Praise the Lord, the mighty King of honor." The "Awakened Ones" of

Würtemburg (typical home of German religious sects)[30] went in for similar exhibitions.

But it was not long before the lofty aspirations of the Reformation called its very opposite into being. The exclusively supernatural tendency was canceled out by a purely "natural" form of reasoning. It is no coincidence that the country which gave the enthusiasm of the Reformation its greatest impetus should also have cradled its reverse. English Deism, which offered human reason a purely natural religion in place of revelation, "might be regarded as a counter-blow to a theology based too much on biblical authority."[31] The doctrine of pure reason, saturated with the conceit of dawning development in the field of natural science and technique, carried its triumphant banner across the Channel and was expanded in France into full-blown rationalism and atheism. Enlightenment, which soon spread to Germany, was the deadly enemy of all revelation and supernatural mysticism. But this is the remarkable thing about it: although the spirit of Enlightenment disagreed with the spirit of Pietism in every respect, yet these two opposites were completely in harmony in their mutual distrust of dogma and their raising of morality in place of religion. It was this spirit more than anything else that gave modern morality its narrow "provincial" character; and this particular brand of morality, replacing the religion of revelation, spread far beyond pietistic circles and succeeded in gaining universal popularity. The ideal of the time was the moral man—never do we come across this expression in literature more than we do during the Age of Enlightenment. Politeness in the sense of being socially correct, a set of rules regulating refinement in living and an outward façade of worldly wisdom were the much-esteemed substitute for positive religion based on dogma. Appropriately enough, one of the most widely read books on moral behavior at that period bears the title *L'honnête homme ou l'art de plaisir à la cour.*[32] The whole purpose of morality was to be complaisant to the mighty, to please the ladies, and to get on well at court. And the whole art of achieving this desirable end was to understand how sexual matters should be handled. But the clue by no means lay in the Christian virtue of chastity! To get on well in good society and make a hit with the ladies, a man had to be capable of acting lasciviously and at the same time appearing to be quite honorable. On this point of outward "honor," of moral "correctness," not only are the puritan of the sixteenth century and the German pietist of the seventeenth century in perfect agreement; but their opposite-numbers, the cavalier of the eighteenth century and the liberal spearhead of the nineteenth century are of exactly the same opinion. The *honnête homme* is the typical figure of social morality, and "moral" becomes a word synonymous with respectable. If he regulated his conduct strictly by Knigges' *Ueber den Umgang mit Menschen,* a man would be perfectly moral and would merit the respect of his fellow men, even though he might trample the whole of the Ten Commandments underfoot. While acknowledging the many valuable qualities that Kant, in his philosophical teachings, brought to bear on the conventions of those characterless times, it is still indisputable that he gave further support to the dominant moral outlook by the very fact that his "ethical religion" provided it with a more solid foundation. Vast numbers of educated people accepted the superficial formula of Kant's teaching without going all the way with their teacher into the deeper aspects of the questions involved. Kant taught that religion in modern times rests solely on ethics; but what Kant did not explain was that ethics only concerns itself with correct outward behavior—the sort of behavior that is scared of causing scandal, but not of committing sin. A man most easily exposes himself to scandal by being discovered in any sexual misdemeanor. Therefore, the sense of the two words "chaste" and "moral" becomes more and more confused till at last, in the nineteenth century, German dictionaries give them an identical meaning. When an "immoral" book is spoken of nowadays, everyone automatically thinks of it as a licentious book; "immoral speech" has come to mean nothing but unchaste speech. This completely distorts the Sixth Commandment. It presents to the mind of the vast, unthinking public an idea of morality quite out of keeping with its real and original meaning; this is morality, a conception linked only with sex; and all the other commandments, with their direct bearing on moral values, are relegated to a position of comparative unimportance. And the worst of it is that this particular emphasis on the Sixth Commandment really relates, in the main, to an outward pattern of honor, while the inner sensibility and modesty of a chaste nature are held up to ridicule and cynical disdain. That is how it came about that in all countries affected by the wave of "Enlightenment" there arose a false morality, for social purposes only, a whited sepulcher affair whose inner rottenness needed the fig leaf of prudery and an elaborate etiquette in sexual matters to cover it up. The meanest adulterer or seducer could be received as a social lion, provided his misdeeds were not publicized. But a man would be considered impossible in good society if he so much as mentioned, even by accident, certain parts of the body, or even articles of clothing, because such crudeness offended the sensitive, who could not bear to be reminded of anything sexual. Our honest trousers became "unmentionables"; our body linen had to be called "undies" or disguised by any other strange-sounding name. Calves or legs were quite indecent, and more intimate parts of the body simply did not exist. What had become of all the ancient simplicity and lack of self-consciousness which, when it found it necessary to speak of these things, gave them their right names? The very naïveté of such conventions was more chaste than all the to-do that accompanies old-maidish simpering and, more often than not, encourages a double life behind the scenes. Is it any wonder that this newer concept led to inherent deceit and produced a tendency among certain people to distrust the whole build-up, impatiently throwing all morality to the winds? Once marriage had become a vehicle for mutual deception, and marital fidelity was turned into rewarding material for comic caricaturists, it is hardly surprising that many people considered it morally better, or at any rate more honest, openly to subscribe to "marriage reform" and "companionate marriages" which at least do not pretend to be anything but what they are. If chastity was only hypocrisy, it was certainly cleaner and more honest to stick to nature than to bolster up all this unnatural squeamishness which preached the self-destruction of the race. If lust was the most powerful and irresistible of all instincts, its satisfaction was also the supreme law of all cohabitation, and birth control consequently could be no crime. Thus, the established attitude toward sexuality became completely confused and sound moral principles were shaken to their very foundation. Harmony turned into turmoil. Millions of fancies, like small floating feathers, were released and taken up by serious thinkers who, seizing their pens, flooded the world with suggestions as to how this chaos could be reduced to order. The sexual question had been born!

Yet the very fact that in circles where the most advanced solutions are advocated, the great care taken to clothe their proposals in the most pleasing colors proves that natural, clear thinking about the fundamental principles of sex life is not yet entirely obsolete, despite all the confusion. That sworn enemy of all puritanism, G. K. Chesterton, placed his finger on the spot in his well-known satirical manner.[33] At one time promiscuous association between the sexes was called "free love"; now it is called "companionate marriage," although it has nothing to do either with comradeship or marriage. Adultery is glossed over as "a marriage mistake," and interference with the unborn receives the almost official title of "birth control." Weak yielding to erotic impulse is allowed to pose as its very opposite, by calling itself "will to live" or even "heightened sensitivity." All these fancy names prove that radical quacks who make a business out of sexual need are, in their heart of hearts, aware of the immorality of their proceedings, because they invariably refrain from calling them that which they really are.

NOTES

1. Xavier von Hornstein and A. Faller, M.D., *Gesundes geschlechtsleben* (Olten, 1950), p. 16.

2. See J. Müller, *Das Sexuelle Leben des Völker* (Paderborn, 1935), p. 148; E. Zeller, *Outlines of the History of Greek Philosophy* (London, 1931); and Jakob Burckhardt, *Kulturgeschichte Griechenland* (abbrev. ed.), p. 539.

3. "Our times, so fruitful in crime, first besmirched the marriage bed; then the family; then the home. That is the fountain from which flow all the sorrows and ills of our nation and people. . . . Our parents, more evil than their's have brought us forth and we are even worse. We shall beget a progeny ecen more vile."

4. L. Friedländer, *Sittengeschichte Roms,* p. 871.

5. Phædrus 246 g–247 d; see H. Meyer, *Geschichte der alten Philosophie* (Munich, 1925), p. 172.

6. *Regulæ brevius tractatæ* 92; PG 31, 1145.

7. See Rufinus, *Historia monachorum* 16; PL 21, 435.

8. For the following, see Hilpisch, *op. cit.*, 67.

9. *Ibid.*, pp. 118, 139, and 155.

10. DB 237, 241–244.

11. See PL 137.

12. The penetrating researches of Peter Browe, S.J., *Beiträge zur Sexualethik des Mittel Alters* (Breslau, 1932), shows that the old heathen superstitions survived well into medieval times, particularly in betrothal and wedding customs. But it also makes clear how much—as, for instance, in the "Tobias Nights" (cf. Tob 8:4) and in wedding ceremonies—they were influenced by Platonic remnants in theology (see especially p. 121). Witchcraft, which became an epidemic in the fourteenth century, set aside many of the old natural concepts and also caused great confusion in ecclesiastical circles. *Maleficium ligationis* played an important role even in theological disputes and ecclesiastical regulations (p. 127).

13. G. Steinhausen, *Geschichte der deutschen Kultur* (Leipzig, 1936), p. 281.

14. Roloff, *Lexikon der Pädagogik*, II, 331, under "Geschlechtliche Aufklärung," mentions that J. J. Rousseau and Tissot at the same time evolved the first system of instructing a child in sexual matters. In Germany, the chief originators of Philanthropy, Basedow, Salzmann and Campe, were responsible for the movement.

15. H. Denifle, O.P., and A. Weiss, O.P., *Luther und Luthertum* (Mainz, 1909), II, 208. [There is a partial translation of this important work available in English, entitled *Luther and Lutheranism* (New York, 1917)—Ed.]

16. DB 367, 401, 424, 428.

17. DB 471, 484.

18. Joannes Janssen, *History of the German People at the Close of the Middle Ages* (St. Louis, 1896–1910), vol. III/IV.

19. DB 788.

20. B. Bartmann, *Lehrbuch der Dogmatik* (Freiburg, 1911), p. 276; Franz Diekamp, *Katholische Dogmatik* (Münster, 1918), p. 140; Denifle-Weiss, *op. cit.*, II, 432 and 497.

21. In his work, *Ehesachen* (Wittenberg, 1530); for literature on this subject, see J. Sägmüller, *Lehrbuch des Kirchenrechts* (Freiburg, 1914), II, 19, note 3.

22. Article, "Sunde," *Die Religion in Geschichte und Gegenwart*, V, 892.

23. *Archiv für Sozialwissenschaften und Sozialpolitik*, XX (1905), 14.

24. *The Social Teaching of the Christian Churches* (New York, n.d.), II, 655.

25. Article, "Puritaner," *Die Religion in Geschichte und Gegenwart*, IV, 1656.

26. The word, *Zimperlich*, which is very often used in the sense of "prude," really has a much wider meaning and is not solely applicable to a timid attitude in sexual matters. It comes from the Middle High Ger-

man, *Zymphirn,* to weep; therefore, tearful, sensitive. [The word is kin to the English, "simper," and has cognates in the various Scandinavian tongues.—Ed.] The word, *Spröde,* "prude," again has a wider sense and connotes coldness and brittleness, just as the term, *Geschämig,* which is confined to certain dialects and can be used in a sympathetic sense. Cf. F. L. K. Weigand, *Deutsches Wörterbuch* (Giessen, 1910).

27. The comprehensive, *Dictionnaire de la langue française ancienne et moderne* by P. Richelet (Paris, 1728) traces the word, *prude,* back to the Latin, *probus* or *prudens.* But in England, at a very early date, it already meant "chaste, honorable," and thus pointed to the sexual sphere, but without any sinister implication. See Skeat, *Etymological Dictionary of the English Language* (Oxford, 1910): "Prude originally used in a good sense—excellent, as in *prudefemme,* a chaste, modest, and honest matron." In France, this added sexual flavor took a long time to establish itself. The *Dictionnaire in trois langues* (Geneva, 1571) defines it as "wise, understanding." The *Dictionnaire française-alemand-latin* by N. Duez (1632) adds to these definitions another, less sympathetic; he describes *pruderie* as *falsa mulierum prudentia,* yet even here the word is not yet limited to the sexual sphere: more properly speaking, it has a witty flavor hinting at the intriguing resourcefulness and cuteness which gives women an advantage over men. Richelet's work, to which we have referred, defined the word completely in its present-day sense. According to him, *pruderie* is feigned, hypocritical virtuousness (*ementita probitas*) and is always associated with women, never with men, as Richelet himself remarks. But even at this time the word's original meaning was not unknown, for the *Deutsch-Französische Wörterbuch* by J. E. Frisch (Leipzig, 1755) defines *pruderie* as denoting wisdom, understanding, piety, but also an affected sense of honor. The English coloring of the word therefore established itself in France about the beginning of the eighteenth century and in Germany even later, about the middle of the eighteenth century. That is why the author feels justified in the line he has taken, tracing it back to the sexual question, and laying the blame for this on the attitude so typical of the English religious sects.

28. A spirited and satisfying definition of the word, "cant," comes from the pen of a distinguished English writer (in consequence of the upheaval of recent times, the author cannot put his hands on the exact reference): "When a German uses the expression, 'cant,' he means a quality which, in the estimation of Continental observers, is a constant and peculiar attribute of the British way of thinking. It differs from hypocrisy in two respects: First, it implies an attempt to justify self-seeking proceedings, by attributing an unselfish motive to them. And secondly, it does not mean that the moral motive is actually either not there, or is not genuine—it simply means that it is not the main motive, and that therefore the particular driving force behind the transaction is not in the least moral. It seems to me that something like this cant does actually exist in the English. It springs from the divided inclination of

the average British soul, to moral rectitude on the one hand, and love of power on the other. In the average Englishman of today the pull of Puritanism is intermingled with the backwash of feudalism. This latter gives him a taste for power, while the Puritan pull supplies him with a Calvinistic conscience. Because the two elements do not mix well, confusion results, and the attempt to cover up this confusion results in cant."

29. *Orthodoxy* (New York, 1936), p. 260; see also J. Sellmair's essay on Chesterton in *Hochland,* XXXV, 211.

30. Cf. J. Scherr, *Deutsche Kultur und Sittengeschichte* (Leipzig, 1929), p. 544.

31. Article, "Deismus," *Die Religion in Geschichte und Gegenwart,* I, 1806.

32. G. Steinhausen, *op. cit.,* p. 479.

33. G. K. Chesterton, *Come to Think of It* (New York, 1931).

CHAPTER 3

The Concept of Morality Within the Church

THE sexual question is one born outside the Church. It is really a by-blow, begotten of the Manichean confusion which, by devaluing all that appertains to the senses and particularly sex, has upset the harmony on which all natural morality is based. A wedge is driven between soul and body, destroying their divinely ordained unity and putting them into a state of mutual antagonism. Two extremes result. On the one hand, we have a feigned "spiritualization" of human nature and, on the other hand, a naked materialism that is incapable of anything above the sensual level.

Now it might be supposed that the fighting attitude Catholics were forced to adopt in the face of the new beliefs would have hindered their ideas from being tinged by puritanical thought. Certainly the polemics of the various confessions underlined their points of difference as emphatically as possible. But the same fighting spirit tended to stimulate emulation. Formal ideas of faith and morality were stepped up so that neither side might appear to be less zealous than its opponents. Hence, even historians like Soldan-Heppe [1] and Riezler [2] admit that it was largely the contention between the various denominations that produced the witch mania which spread as rapidly as an epidemic because neither party was willing to be behindhand in its zeal for the faith. The confusion in the case of Galileo can be explained by a similar infection, the one-sided veneration of the Bible in its literal sense having found acceptance even in Catholic circles, so that the seventeenth century suspected as unbiblical heresies things which had been hailed as scientific discoveries a whole century earlier. Ecclesiastical authorities found it quite proper to condemn the teachings of Copernicus who had been permitted to propagate them openly in his own time, and even to dedicate his book to Pope Paul III in 1543. The same touchy attitude (to quote a more homely example) was also responsible for the substitution of biblical names for the good old German Christian names which had served for centuries. One can confirm this by a glance at the older memorial tablets where even names taken from the Bible or the Calendar of Saints were transmuted into German spelling, to make them sound less foreign. Hans, Veit Jörg, Lisbet, Bärbel, are typical examples. Puritanism replaced them with names from the Old Testament; German Protestantism preferred to draw from the New, or turned good German names into Latin. Homemade, pietistic names like Fear-God, Trust-God, Praise-God,[3] and so on, were also not despised. It was universally regarded as impious not to use Christian names that were either taken from the Bible or had an uplifting sound. So the German names disappeared more and more, even among Catholics, and names tended to take on that uniform character that persists among Catholics and Protestants alike, even to this day.

In the sphere of sexual morality the influence was

even stronger. Neither side wanted to be outdone by the other in moral correctness because each had a particularly sharp eye for any failings in the opposite camp, in order thereby to produce an argument proving the superiority of their own faith and the falsity of the opponents. Split up into several armies, no longer regarding one another as blood brothers in faith, they became deadly enemies; and this took its own revenge in the most frightful way because religion became a party question. This party struggle, like any other militant undertaking, adopted warlike methods, which meant that individual questions of religion and morality were no longer determined by truth-principles but by expediency. Apologetics became more important than dogma. This inevitably led to some truths being more, or some less, emphatically stressed. Here the Catholic side had the advantage because, thanks to the authority of the sacred college and the cohesion of the one, universal Church, distortion of this kind could not affect the fundamental substance of faith. Critics had to confine their attack to the personal application of the Church's teaching to life as a whole. The principles as such necessarily remained untouched.

In personal exchanges with non-Catholics and in many competent writings, one often meets with prejudice, as if the Church represented Manichean views, by condemning woman, by declaring marriage unclean, and by pronouncing the human body sinful.[4] Some of these beliefs spring from regrettable ignorance of the Church's teachings; others spring from a spiteful readiness to besmirch the opponent and speak ill of him on every possible occasion. But even among serious critics the reproach recurs again and again. Undoubtedly, it at least bears out the conviction that Manichean teachings are chiefly to blame for the present-day confusion in sexual ethics.

But to ascribe such lunacy to the Catholic Church, and even to look upon it as a dogma of the Church, is not only a fatal error but also a downright injustice.

There is no difficulty in disposing of this error. Not only has the Church never set up such a dogma but, on the contrary, it has waged relentless warfare against Manicheism right through the ages and at one time succeeded in vanquishing it completely. One can quote innumerable instances of the uncompromising attitude the Church took whenever Manichean ideas cropped up again. In older days there were the Spanish and Gallic Synods against Priscillian and the Manicheans; [5] in the Middle Ages there were the energetic proceedings against the Albigensians, the Fraticelli, and the Beguines.[6] All these stressed the sanctity of marriage. More modern times produced the important decisions on original sin and justification enacted at the fifth and sixth sessions of the Council of Trent. This made absolutely clear the view of the Church, that the nature of man was not completely ruined, but only weakened by original sin. The very people who make fun of dogmatic "hairsplitting" should see clearly by this example how necessary exact phraseology is in formulating axiomatic principles, and how an apparently negligible difference of expression can distort a sense, causing the whole outlook on the world to be sharply divided by opposing views. The educational authority of the Church has never missed an opportunity of repudiating Manichean ideas or similar notions, branding them unequivocally as the heresies they are.

Nevertheless, we cannot allow ourselves to rest content with our self-satisfying apologetics. Truth, humility, and love of our adversaries force us to penetrate more deeply into the question—how it can come about that, despite the official and emphatic stand the Church has repeatedly taken, there are still so many who have the false impression that contempt of marriage and sexual morality, and a Manichean attitude of enmity towards nature, are tenets of our faith. It is perfectly true that, despite the definite ruling of the Church, certain undercurrents actually are present within the Church and do suggest preoccupation with the spiritual at the expense of the senses' claims. The true Catholic has at all times emphatically rejected materialism, but the same energetic vigilance has not invariably been applied to its other extreme; on the contrary, in materialistic times, when the world has been very partial to the satisfaction of the senses, it is not surprising that the pious believer has yielded enthusiastically to a pull in the opposite direction. We have already seen in the previous chapter that, in the early Church, even distinguished thinkers like Origen, Tertullian, and for a time St. Augustine himself, were unable to resist the lure of "spiritualizing" systems. If such minds could be ensnared, how much more must the ordinary mentality be attracted to a way of life that promises so much. Naturally, it must seem that a man's moral status rises in proportion to his spiritual mastery; the more he detaches his soul from earthly things, the more drastically he denies himself all sensual pleasures, the more perfect he becomes. The keynote of the *Imitation of Christ* (I, 25), "in tantum proficies, in quantum tibi ipse vim intuleris" —"your progress will be in proportion to the discipline you exercise over yourself"—was at all times taken literally, and without any necessary qualifications, in pious Catholic circles. It implied that if good works were difficult, they increased in merit—as if the harder the treatment visited upon the body, the greater would be the benefit to the soul.[7] To people with "idealism," every concession to the body, no matter how necessary, appears a regrettable compromise, a yielding to the senses. The necessity is a thing under which a human being suffers, and to which the idealist yields only with the greatest reluctance and repugnance. By this process of reasoning the senses are branded as utterly inferior. If even great brains like Plato's have been caught in the trap hidden in this logical short cut, one really cannot wonder that more superficial thinkers have failed to notice the error which arises from a false, and therefore unnatural, presupposition. The body and the senses express the Creator's positive will just as much as the soul and the spiritual. Even though the senses must be subordinated to the spirit, they were still created by God and are therefore good, as the Scriptures emphasize in the very first chapter. According to the teachings of the Church (DB 787) and the exact analysis of St. Thomas Aquinas (*Sum. Th.*, 1-2, q. 85, a. 1), the nature of man was in no way altered or diminished by original sin. St. Thomas teaches that the sum total of man's nature, and all that is its due, namely, reason and free will, was not dissolved or lessened by original sin, but there was a decline in its aspiration toward virtue (*inclinatio ad virtutem*). A limiting influence set in, affecting its direction and attraction to the highest good, with the result that the power of man's free will, though not destroyed, no longer acted as it formerly did, in harmony with and under the guidance of spiritual grace. The injury, therefore, lies more in its relationship to that supernatural aspiration and order which was the divine intention at the creation. The loss of supernatural grace meant a tragic deterioration in the route by which all mankind must reach its ultimate goal.

It follows that divine order cannot consist of a biased suppression of the senses for the benefit of the spirit; it must lie in a harmonized coordination of both. Exaggerated spiritualism is just as dangerous as materialism. It can, in fact, be even more perilous to high-minded, pious individuals who are eagerly striving for perfection, just because it is more closely related to truth and outwardly very often resembles it. Spiritualism will always have a certain advantage and, therefore, prove all the more convincing in cases where ascetic leanings are not guided by clear revelation, but depend for their impetus on personal reasoning. Radical proceedings will always make a stronger appeal than moderation to those who do not think deeply; total abstinence, to these, will seem more laudable than mere sobriety because they tend to regard all moderation as moral weakness, a yielding to half measures. All the false directions that beset the path of true believers are less deluding than that of spiritualism, just because it gives itself the airs of idealism and therefore makes a particularly pompous impression. The Church at all times has had a great deal of trouble from this source; and one can hardly wonder that exaggerated spiritualism was particularly in evidence about the time of the Reformation when it worked all the more destructively because pious believers simply could not tolerate the idea that their opponents, who were so inordinately proud of their moral superiority, should be more "spiritual" than they were.

The one-time "Old Catholic" priest, Father K. Jentsch, wrote in 1900 in the weekly publication *Jugend,* which could never be suspected of exceptional sympathy toward the Church, "One cannot deny that the Church gave aesthetic education in the North its first impetus. Then came the Reformation with its attack upon pictorial art and the Puritans completed the destruction. The Catholic hierarchy took the alarm; it was scared of being accused of immorality and started a campaign against the 'heathenish' in Art. The liberal professor, important citizen and good paterfamilias is a pattern of correct behavior and fosters ridiculous prudery (except of course at stag parties). One can hardly wonder that priests, if only for the sake of their reputation, could not be backward in their zeal for morality." [8] The spirit that animates this effusion is obvious; and of course one must not confuse the author's "hierarchy" with the educational authority of the Church—but at any rate, such expressions of opinion illustrate the venom of the opposing parties and at the same time their zeal to leave nothing undone that might prove their high sense of morality. That such unmeasured zeal should lead to distortions and abortions was inevitable. It was equally impossible that the tensions between the extremes of Pietism and Rationalism, between Puritanism and Naturalism, should fail to have some repercussions on Catholics living in the same community with these ardent Reformers and constantly exposed to the influence they exerted. Unconsciously, they found themselves shunted onto the same dangerous lines which hurried the *Zeitgeist* along. Morality was set above religion; religion became merely a prop for a "moral change of life." The uplifting pamphlets of the time are just one succession of edifying tales with the more trite and obvious "morals" to point their purpose. The "moral man," the "philanthropist," only in a more pious guise, also became the Catholic ideal, to be extolled from countless pulpits during the Age of Enlightenment. And this inevitably degenerated into more and more veneration of chastity, to the overshadowing of all the other virtues. Increasingly, the word chastity was used as a synonym for morality as a whole.

Although an empty, feigned morality, which studied only the outward forms of good behavior, no matter what lusts they might conceal, was never tolerated by

Catholics nor, for that matter, by sincere Protestants either; still, even here a tendency arose to place sexual conventions as the standard of all that was honorable and correct—in the forefront where ethics was concerned. The unthinking masses readily adopted the amalgamation of "chaste" and "moral" which the Puritans had been the first to sponsor. Eventually, this usage spread to educated circles which really should have known better.

Of course, the change of meaning never became completely universal. To this day there is a yawning gulf between the word "morality" as used in the language of science and the same word when employed by the general public. Ask any layman, even among the cultured, what he means by the word "immoral" and, in nine cases out of ten, the answer will refer to sexual misdemeanor, with not a hint of the other moral spheres the meaning is supposed to cover. "Public morality" is a concept which never recalls to the average mind offenses like profiteering, cheating, or slander; whereas "crimes against morality" are regarded simply as sexual offenses, leaving out of account altogether sins against life and property. We use the word in the same limited sense when we talk about immoral pictures, immoral dances, immoral plays or books.

This use of the word is quite foreign to the official language of science. Textbooks on moral theology define morality as the sum total of all questions, and consequently they only use the word "moral" or "immoral" in this universal, natural sense. The sexual aspect is only one section of the vast complex of morality, and not even the most important section. Only very seldom do we find the word used in the popular sense, as, for instance, once only in the *Handbook on Christian Morality* by the famous Professor Sailer (Vol. II, p. 50), or in

Göpfert's[9] book on moral theology (Vol. II, 5, p. 342). Göpfert uses it twice in the universal sense, but in such a way that the sexual significance is uppermost. Scientists as a whole take very little notice of the fact that, apart from its universal and scientific application, the word has taken on another, and very much narrower, meaning to the general public. The first man to call attention to this change of meaning seems to have been the cultural historian G. Grupp.[10] J. Mausbach, in the *Kirchlichen Handlexikon* (II, p. 2120), confirms that, apart from the accepted concept of morality, a narrower, vulgar usage exists which limits the meaning of this word to "duitful behavior in all that appertains to sexual life," but he does not venture any opinion as to whether such a limitation is permissible or not. O. Schilling also calls attention to it in his textbook on moral theology (II, 377) and in *Lexikon für Theologie und Kirche* (IX, 605, *s.v.,* "Sittlichkeit").

Preachers and teachers, however, were not so conservative in approaching the vulgar use of the word. This may have been partly due to the fact that in their profession they were not morally bound to use scientific language; on the contrary, much of their success might depend upon their being able to meet their hearers on common ground by using words the great masses were familiar with. But even they adapted themselves to current usage only late in the day and with a certain amount of hesitation. Anyone who carefully examines old sermons, from the Middle Ages down to comparatively modern times, must be struck by the fact that the word "immoral" scarcely ever appears even in its universal sense, and is not used at all with the limited meaning of the present day. When great medieval preachers like Berthold of Ratisbon, Johann Geiler von Kaysersberg, and so on, wanted to emphasize sins against social order, they used expressions like lewdness, prostitution, licentiousness, lust, cunning, brazen and scandalous behavior. Berthold reserves for this class of sinner the term *Näscher,*[11] in a sense no longer in common currency, implying one "who goes in for illicit pleasure"; and Abraham a Sancta Clara, in his own blunt fashion, calls their proceedings "bestial." If we thoroughly examine the works of a vast number of old-time preachers and religious authors like, for example, J. Janssen, whose *History of the German People* is well known, H. Denifle in his work on Luther, and even the Protestant R. Cruel in his *History of German Sermons of the Middle Ages* (Detmold, 1879), we do not once come across the word "immoral" to describe sexual offenses, even where these authors occupy themselves exclusively with sexual matters. Two conclusions must surely be drawn from this fact. First, that the use of the word in this sense is of comparatively recent date, which bears out the argument we set forth above; and secondly, that it crept into Catholic pulpit usage a long time after the Age of Enlightenment—that is to say, after the general public had accepted it—and therefore much hesitation and thought must have taken place before the word was accepted inside the Church. Even toward the end of the eighteenth and the first half of the nineteenth century, one seldom comes across it in Catholic sermons. The great collections of F. X. Sailer (*Festpredigten,* Augsburg, 1770), A. Kern (*Predigten auf alle Sonn- und Festtage des Jahres,* Augsberg, 1783), F. K. Felder (*Christliche Reden,* Ulm, 1809), J. Schneller (*Predigten auf alle Sonntage des Jahres,* Augsburg, 1787) contain not one instance of the word being used in its modern sense. It occurs once only in Bishop Colmar of Mainz's well-known sermons, which were published by his friends (Mainz, 1838), and even that one occurrence is in connection with a speech on mortal sin (Vol. III, p. 187). One searches for it in vain even in the vast and varied crop of sermons that appeared in succeeding years; for instance, those of B. von Wermelskirchen, Königsdorfer, Zollner, among others. We first find it in G. Busl's *Katechetischen Predigten,* a book much used in South Germany, where the author uses it three times in dealing with the Sixth Commandment; but even he uses words like unchastity, impurity, shamelessness.

So we see that the use of the word immorality to denote sexual misdemeanors, as we commonly use it today, is a comparatively recent innovation, one which has crept in only during the last century. In fact, one might say that its universal acceptance today is really a chapter in the literary history of the last few decades. This is all the more remarkable because the word "moral" was a special favorite during the Age of Enlightenment, and is to be found again and again in classical works of that period. The fact that it occurs so seldom in Catholic sermons [12] of that time surely suggests that preachers suspected the word of having acquired a meaning which did not quite square up with the Catholic view of morality.

Nowadays, the change of meaning finds universal acceptance and is used in our own sermons, textbooks, and catechisms without any reflection. The practice has not yet become quite so common in serious works of theology; with very few exceptions, these reflect a greater conservatism and also a more exact appreciation of the word's true meaning.

In the erstwhile *Lehrbuch der Katholische Religion für die oberen Klassen höherer Lehranstalten* [13] (III, p. 58), sins against chastity are defined as "everything that offends against divine order in the moral sphere"—as if crimes like slander and dishonesty no longer fell within the meaning of moral sphere! Of course, here, as in most cases, it is a matter of falling in with popular usage, the common speech of the people having long since adopted the change in the meaning of morality, thus making an established fact of the limited meaning, a fact with which the ecclesiastical organ has to reckon. But it is worth noting that its employment in such a work gives the official seal of approval to a usage which was formerly prohibited.

Discrepancies in legal language give further confirmation of the change of meaning that has gradually insinuated itself. The *Bürgerliches Gesetzbuch* (civil code), in paragraphs 138, 1568, 1666, 2333 abs. 5, and 2336, speaks of "immoral behavior"; but B. Plank, in his explanations,[14] emphasizes that chronic alcoholism, gambling, vagabondage, etc., as well as licentiousness, are covered by "immoral behavior." So the *Bürgerliches Gesetzbuch* uses the word in its original, universal sense. The *Strafgesetzbuch* (penal code), on the other hand, in the title of the thirteenth section, "Crimes and Trespasses against Morality"—as well as in sections 184 and 235, where it speaks of "segregation from the public on account of gainful or immoral purposes"—uses it in the narrow, vulgar sense. Perhaps lawyers are not quite blameless of introducing the word into common currency; and it is worth noting that to the average lawyer the word morality is a very relative conception, having a close connection with the word mores. Thus the well-known specialist on legal matters, F. v. Liszt, who enjoyed an enormous reputation among his colleagues, in his *Lehrbuch des deutschen Strafrechts,*[15] described morality as "the confining of sexual behavior within the limits of current mores."

Habits and customs are capable of changing at any time, but the essential principles of morality are unchangeable, for habits and customs adapt themselves to the peculiarities of a race, to a particular climate, or to religion; whereas morality (in its original, universal sense) rests on the unalterable will of God, formulated as natural laws in the Decalogue and rooted in every individual conscience. Actually, this juggling has brought about the false conception which, treating morality as a product of folk custom, makes it subject to the changing influences of time and race. If it is true that speech is the mirror of thought and judgment, this change of meaning cannot be written off as a mere question of historical evolution. The narrower meaning the word has taken on must be the expression of a corresponding contraction in human thought because of the mental image it reflects. Superficially, this may sound like a mere play on words, but deeper reflection will show that the matter really does touch the innermost nature of morality. From the very fact of the modern conception limiting this word to only one section of morality, we arrive at two inescapable conclusions—first, that morality relates to sexual behavior, as if that were the only standard by which a man's character could be judged; and secondly, that all other branches of morality, like social duty, honesty, loyalty, truth, are pushed into the background of moral consciousness and sometimes completely obscured. This means that the hypertrophy of the sexual, which for years has set its seal on our private lives and to some extent on public life as well, is the real source of the sexual question.

There is no doubt that many who make use of this word, for instance, Catholic preachers and all who occupy official positions, do so only because it has entrenched itself so deeply in popular language. It never occurs to any of them literally to dilute the word's meaning; still, there is an objective division between speech and thought. And there is always the danger that such a form of expression may unconsciously lead to thought processes which cast a doubt on the original and natural meaning of morality, especially as an unbridled flirtation with spiritualism may lead a person astray in the same direction. The modern use of the word morality conjures up the idea that things sexual are morality's chief concern and that this also expresses its compass in a theological sense—in other words, that chastity is the most important of all virtues, and unchastity the most heinous sin.

This idea has succeeded in gaining a very wide acceptance, even in Catholic circles. "Chastity, the Queen of Virtues" has become a stock phrase, very much favored by magazines of an uplifting character designed for the young, and in publications issued by some religious denominations. The well-known priest A. von Doss, so esteemed as a writer for young people, in his work *Pearl among the Virtues,*[16] writes: "Where purity is lacking, everything falls short—for this is the most essential, the most valuable and the very highest quality." "Purity is the pearl of pearls, for all the other virtues derive their value and their luster from purity alone." The whole of the book is concerned with the elaboration of this idea which, incidentally, is also much in evidence in the same author's other well-known work, his *Thoughts and Counsels for Catholic Young Men.* Another well-known author, Alban Stolz, speaks of chastity as "the sum-total of a moral life" and declares a breach of the Sixth Commandment to be "truly the most grievous of all sins." [17] Prince Bishop Johann Zwerger of Seckau represents the same view in his book, *The Most Beautiful Virtue and the Ugliest Crime.*[18] His attitude will be seen at once, even from the chapter headings: "Unchastity the Most Shameful Vice"; "The Dangerous Vice"; "The Vice

God Hates Most"; "The Vice God Punishes Most." The collections of sermons issued by Busl and Zollner,[19] which are very widely used in South Germany, spread the same teaching. Both make a point of quoting St. Bernard: "If a man gives himself over to pride he certainly sins—but only [!] in the manner of an angel; if he yields to greed, he is certainly trespassing, but in the manner of a man. If, however, he gives way to the impure lusts of the flesh, he sins like a beast" (Zollner). Similarly, Busl says: "Every vice stains the soul, but nothing does more to disfigure it than unchastity. That is why this vice is called impure, the sin of impurity. Pride is the sin of angels, greed the sin of man, but lust is the sin of brute animals." It should be noted here that neither of these quotations represents St. Bernard, either verbally or by implication, for the teachings of St. Bernard were quite contrary to this spirit, as will be shown below. The same ideas are represented in the scarcely less popular collection of sermons by J. Frassinetti.[20] "This evil [unchastity] is the ugliest and most repugnant vice than can defile a man, the most chronic cancer of the soul. It is the summit of all evil." The most emphatic pronouncement comes from Hunolt, the preacher of the cathedral of Trier. Hunolt belongs to an earlier period, but his sermons carry weight even at the present time, and are constantly being reissued.

In his thirteenth and fourteenth sermons[21] he describes unchastity as the most wicked of all vices. "There is no vice that offends God more than that of impure love"—he even maintains (harking back to Tertullian) that "unchastity is worse than the renunciation of Faith" (p. 257). We may look upon Hunolt as the first pioneer of this teaching in Catholic homilies. Further on we shall have to refer to him again in this connection.

This selection of quotations, which shows how widespread the habit of representing unchastity as the greatest crime against morality has already become, could be still further extended. Most of the examples are taken from the period of our parents and grandparents; that is to say, they belong to an era in the history of homiletics sufficiently well known for a trend toward moralizing which is no longer in vogue. It would, nevertheless, be a mistake to believe that the underlying thought has also disappeared. Nowadays, the pendulum swings just as dynamically between the extremes of puritanical prudery and neopagan licentiousness as it did in all other periods of overcivilization and decline. The plethora of literature on sexual enlightenment, which is even to be found on Catholic bookshelves, proves that we are still far from the calm security of our pious medieval forefathers who accepted as a matter of course such facts as conception, birth, and relationship within the marriage bond. The effects of World War I and the period that preceded it have, in regard to this particular problem, penetrated even to the tiniest village. At one time, one could estimate the moral status of a parish by the number of its illegitimate births, but nowadays that standard is totally meaningless. No one could be so naïve as to regard this decline as a mark of progress. Immorality and perversion, which were formerly exclusively associated with the loose life of big cities, have now spread over the length and breadth of the land, and can be traced with the most staggering certainty in the enormous number of youthful, or even childish, offenders against sexual propriety. Preachers therefore have every right to deal with the problem as one of the most unmistakable signs of degeneration among the people—but the important thing is to discover the most effective method of attack. Many an earnest preacher may consider it his first duty to use direct methods: by showing up this moral pestilence from the pulpit as often and as drastically as possible. But this has the disadvantage of laying disproportionate importance on the Sixth Commandment and elevating it above all the others, which would appear to give it a practical, even if not a dogmatic, primacy in moral questions. It is because of this that many theologians feel justified in calling chastity the "Queen" (that is to say the most important) of virtues, and in putting morality and chastity on the same footing; in adopting this line they are actuated by purely tactical motives. One highly esteemed philosophical-theological periodical energetically takes their part by saying: "The expression is a perfectly correct one owing to the fact that in the sphere of chastity many [God knows how many!] find the dictum fitting for their state of faith and grace." [22] Another theological publication justifies the description of chastity as the most important virtue by the following: "Even if chastity is essentially less important than brotherly love, it still, by its particular nature and properties, merits the very particular cherishing it receives at the hands of mature, enlightened preachers." [23]

Of course, no one would dispute that chastity merits especially careful cherishing. But the question is whether it really deserves first place—to be valued and set above all other virtues. The teachings of the gospel and the teachings of the Church give it a different valuation in the moral sphere.

NOTES

1. Soldan-Heppe, *Geschichte der Hexenprozesse* (Stuttgart, 1880), I, 429.

2. S. Riezler, *Geschichte der Hexenprozesse in Bayern* (Stuttgart, 1896), pp. 127 and 141.

3. Steinhausen, *op. cit.*, pp. 68, 262 and 415.

4. Many proofs of this in F. Walter, *Der Leib und sein Recht im Christentum* (Donauwörth, 1910); Forel-Fetscher, *Die Sexuelle Frage* (Munich, 1931), p. 367; *Arztblatt für Bryern,* 14 (1936), 237. We meet this reproach particularly often in J. Marcuse, *Die Sexuelle Frage und das Christentum* (Leipzig, 1908), pp. 11, 35, 47, etc., who also, by the way, speaks of Luther's *sola fides* teaching as a Catholic dogma (p. 9). And it is moreover interesting that many of these critics prove themselves to be not entirely free from Manichean ways of thinking. The Berlin sexual-psychologist, A. Kind, in *Blätter für Bibliophile* (March, 1908), says, "Anything that is calculated to stimulate the natural and acquired erotic reactions psychologically, is obscene" (cited in Forel-Fetscher). And Nietzsche, despite his sharp objection to all who "despise the body" cannot deny that he is subject to similar thought-processes. He exceeds even the most rabid medieval ascetic in his abhorrence of womankind as a creation of evil. "Woman is indescribably more wicked than man, and cleverer also. In a woman goodness is already a sign of *degeneration*" (*Ecce Homo,* "Why I Write Such Excellent Books," 5).

5. DB 236, 241, 244.

6. DB 402, 424, 471, 477.

7. The *Imitation of Christ* has also been reproached with advocating escape from the world in an absolute sense, although this is unjust. Because it was written for monastic orders it lays emphasis on asceticism, but a number of passages prove that it does not look upon asceticism in a spiritualistic way; it follows the law of harmony laid down by St. Benedict. Particularly is this clear in Book III, Chapter 38: "My son you ought diligently to aim at this, that in every place, and in every action or outward occupation, you be *inwardly* free and master of yourself; that all things be under you, and not you under them; and that you be lord and ruler of your actions, and not a slave or a hireling. Rather you should be a freeman and a true Hebrew, transferred to the lot and *liberty of the sons of God.* They stand *above things present,* and contemplate the eternal; *with the left eye they regard transitory things, and with the right those of heaven.* Temporal things draw them not away to cleave to them; *but they rather draw these things so that they may subserve aright the end* for which they were ordained by God and appointed by that Sovereign Artist, who has left nothing disordered in His whole creation." And similarly, Book III, Chapter 26: "It is not lawful to cast it all away, for nature must be sustained; but to require superfluities, and such things as are rather for delight, Thy holy law forbids; for then the flesh would rebel against the spirit. In all this, I beseech Thee, let Thy hand govern and teach me, that there may be no excess."

8. *Jugend,* II (1900), 502.

9. J. Göttler, *Geschichte der Pedagogik* (Berlin, 1921), p. 129.

10. The author gratefully acknowledges that Prof. O. Schilling called this fact to his attention in a review of the earlier edition in *Tübingen Theologische Quartalschrift,* I/II (1932).

11. J. and W. Grimm's *Deutsches Wörterbuch* defines *Näscher* as one who enjoys dainties, one who indulges in dainties frequently, and also, in a direct reference to Brother Berthold, "one who is unchaste."

12. It would be most interesting to examine Protestant collections of sermons with the object of tracing the word back in the same way; unfortunately, the present author was not able to do this.

13. In its original version, the *Lehrbuch* did not contain these wide-ranging expressions. These distorting words were incorporated in later, revised editions. The *Lehrbuch* is now no longer in use.

14. *Bürgerliches Gesetzbuch,* V, 856.

15. F. von Liszt, *Lehrbuch des deutschen Strafrechts,* X (Berlin, 1900), 347.

16. (Mainz, 1888), pp. 8 and 94; English translation, Baltimore, n.d.

17. A. Stolz, *Erziehungskunst* (Freiburg, 1891), p. 104.

18. Graz, 1898.

19. G. Busl, *Katechetische Predigten,* II, 666; J. E. Zollner, *Das Katholische Christentum, Katechismuspredigten von den Geboten,* I, 405.

20. *Das Evangelium des Herrn dem Volke Erklärt* (Munich, 1908), IV, 114; a translation from the Italian.

21. *Sermons* (New York, 1888-1896), vol. III.

22. *Scholastik,* IV (1931).

23. *Zeitschrift für katholische Theologie* (1922), p. 440.

CHAPTER 4

Literature and Documents Relating to the Moral Concept

TEACHINGS which give the impression that chaste behavior is the summit of morality, and define unchastity as the greatest moral offense, undoubtedly arise from the best intentions, their underlying motive being to arrest the flood of licentiousness that threatens to engulf humanity. Both in clerical circles and among the general public, they have produced a conviction that there is nothing more urgent in the care of souls than to guard against sexual offenses. All other problems are thereby rendered comparatively unimportant and are consigned to the background.

A glance at scriptural sources, at the teachings of the early fathers, and at theological literature down the centuries should suffice to make this attitude untenable.

It must be clear to everyone that the term "morality" applies to moral teaching as a whole and takes in, not only the Sixth, but all of the Ten Commandments. By mentioning one out of ten, undue emphasis is bound to be laid on it, for when a thing is singled out for special mention it is automatically impressed upon the mind to the exclusion of every other part of the context (*denominatio fit a potiori*).

The whole question boils down to this: which is the most important commandment in the compass of morality? Asked "Which is the greatest of all commandments?" Christ our Lord answered: "Thou shalt love the Lord thy God with thy whole heart . . . and thy neighbor as thyself" (Mark 12: 30; Luke 10: 27). Love in its indivisible duality, love of God and brotherly love, is the mark of every disciple of Christ (John 13: 34); it is the norm to which God directs all mankind.

Apostolic teaching expresses the same principle. "Love is the fulfilling of the law" (Rom. 13: 10), "is the bond of perfection" (Col. 3: 14), is the imitation of God (Eph. 5: 1). It is the highest of all divine qualities; therefore it must necessarily be more important than all the other virtues. "And now there remain faith, hope and charity, these three; but the greatest of these is charity" (I Cor. 13: 13). Despite all the harsh things he has to say about lewdness, it is, on the other hand, precisely St. Paul who again and again extols charity as the highest virtue, rating it mountain-high above faith, more precious than voluntary poverty, preferable to the most painful martyrdom, and weightier than the proclaiming of the truth with the tongues of men and of angels.

True, the same apostle excommunicated the man of Corinth who gave scandal to the whole community by his vice. It is also St. Paul who says that the much overworked term for unchastity should not be mentioned at all by Christians, as it is unfit for use among holy men and women. In all the sermons on impurity, the word is used in a half-veiled way so that the shame of this sin may not be emphasized unduly—but very few notice that the whole passage covers not only unchastity but also applies to vices like greed and foolish or ill-considered utterances. "But fornication and all uncleanness or covetousness, let it not be so much as named among you, as becometh saints; or obscenity or foolish talking or scurrility which is to no purpose" (Eph. 5: 3-4). Of all the writers of the inspired Scriptures, St. Paul is perhaps the one who most violently attacks loose behavior. One can well understand that his mission in the vicious Mediterranean cities, where decaying Hellenic culture, mingled with the degenerate backwash of declining Asiatic civilization, made this very necessary. But not even he ever suggests that unchastity is the most heinous of all sins. He of all the scriptural authors is the one who gave love the primacy in his song of praise extolling it to the skies. In his homilies to the primitive Christian communities, he stresses the importance of love time and again, making it the cornerstone of all morality, the very first quality a Christian must possess above all others. "Owe no man anything, but to love one another. For he that loveth his neighbor hath fulfilled the law" (Rom. 13: 8).

St. Peter also makes love of one's neighbor the first and most important duty, more urgent even than watching and praying. "But before all things have a constant mutual charity among yourselves" (I Peter 4: 8). There is scarcely any need to emphasize that charity is the dominant theme of the letters written by St. John, the apostle of love.

If the description "Queen of Virtues" or "Pearl of Virtues" is permitted at all, it should undoubtedly apply to love; and whoever, even with the best intentions, assigns this term to any other virtues is guilty of dethroning charity by shifting the moral accent from the true center to the circumference. The truly moral man, in the strictest sense, is the man aglow with divine love. If Jesus Christ and the apostles made this the norm of a morality that fulfilled the whole law, we have no right whatsoever to set up another standard by which morality can be judged. The love of God and of our neighbor must be the standard by which we, as Christians, measure our own ideals and—as far as that is permissible—the ideals of our neighbors. The Holy Scriptures are absolutely clear and definite on this point, and leave no possible room for any doubt, either in theory or in practice. That also means that, in the ironing out of the relative importance of love and chastity, there is no possible room for any roundabout way of avoiding the "problem," which really is no problem at all. "So far as the connection between chastity and love is concerned, in actual practice, there seems to us no better solution than the one suggested by our Lord on one occasion when faced with a similar proposition, namely: 'You shall do this one thing, and not leave this other thing undone.' The case is not served by favoritism and exaggeration." [1] Clearly, chastity is a most important part of morality as a whole, and can no more afford to be neglected than other virtues, like justice, truthfulness, and so on. It may even happen in practice that under certain circumstances chastity must be singled out for special attention, just as, on another occasion, it may be necessary to single out one of the other virtues for particularly urgent reasons. But such exceptions by no means alter the rule, nor do they provide any excuse for raising chastity permanently to an equality with love, or even pretending that it is superior to charity itself, since our Lord, by His own teachings, has shown us exactly where the chief emphasis belongs.

Much of the confusion on this point may arise from the fact that the concepts of love and of morality are not always viewed in sharp focus. The love of which our Lord speaks, and which the apostles praise so highly, is something altogether different from the emotions so gaudily depicted in modern romances, plays, and films. Probably no other word or concept in the language is so misunderstood or so misused as love. Some people are quite satisfied that it means nothing more than compassion and mercy toward the weak and the ailing; but that is only one of the many forms and functions of love. Others give the word a still narrower interpretation by confining it solely to sex and, even in this sphere, to pure emotion—love in their estimation is yearning or straining for stupendous effects. But emotion is really only a by-product which may be lacking completely in the most precious love of all—that love which calls for heroic self-sacrifice or sober, everyday performance of duty. Nor does love consist solely of the performance of good works on this, that, or the other humanitarian ground. Even the complete abandonment of all personal possessions for the benefit of the poor is not love itself—it can indeed miss the true essence of love, as the apostle points out (I Cor. 13: 3).

In the Holy Scriptures the word charity has a very broad meaning. But three essentials stand out clearly:

1. The love of God toward man, which is revealed first and foremost in the eternal mystery of Christ (true God and true man) and His salvation, the fruit of which is the supernatural lifting up of man. Here *caritas* equals healing grace "which is poured forth in our hearts, by the Holy Ghost who is given to us" (Rom. 5: 5).

2. Man's answer to this: the complete and utter surrender of the whole heart, the whole soul, the whole mind, and the whole strength, which expresses itself outwardly in doing God's will by true obedience to the divine commandments. "For this is the charity of God: that we keep his commandments" (I John 5: 3).

3. The love men should bear toward one another, insofar as it does not spring from natural motives, but is

grounded in love of God, the Creator, and Christ, the Head; this is *caritas fraternitatis*—"Let the charity of brotherhood abide in you" (Heb. 13: 1)—which Christ proclaimed as the commandment of the New Covenant (John 13: 34). This is the sign by which disciples may be recognized (John 13: 35), and which St. Paul describes as being more important than faith or martyrdom (I Cor. 13: 1).

The essential and most marvelous thing about these three aspects of charity, however, is that they do not exist as separate kinds of love running parallel, but constitute one complete and indissoluble trinity in unity, which nothing can change and which goes on for all eternity. Endlessly they are renewed in organic combination by the Creator Himself. "And the second is like to it: Thou shalt love thy neighbor as thyself." The Beloved Disciple gives the most beautiful explanation of this trinity in unity in the words: "By this hath the charity of God appeared towards us because God hath sent his only-begotten Son into the world that we may live by him. In this is charity—not as though we had loved God, but because he hath first loved us and sent his Son to be a propitiation for our sins. My dearest, if God hath so loved us, we also ought to love one another. If we love one another God abideth in us: and his charity is perfected in us" (I John 4: 9-11). This unique interrelationship of the essence of love is also expressed very forcibly by St. Paul in his epistle in praise of this virtue (I Cor. 13). He speaks of love as an eternal quality, outlasting even faith and hope; but he ascribes to charity qualities which chiefly affect our neighbor: "Charity is patient, is kind; charity envieth not, dealeth not perversely, is not puffed up . . . beareth all things, believeth all things, hopeth all things, endureth all things; charity never falleth away."

St. Thomas Aquinas also emphasizes the quality of love of God and one's neighbor as an essential, numerical unity. Love of God and love of one's neighbor are not two separate virtues, but one and the same. In the *Summa* (2-2, q. 23, a. 5: *Utrum caritas sit una virtus*), he refutes the contention that love of one's neighbor is a thing quite distinct and separate from love of God, by pointing out that this is an illusion; what actually happens is that when we love our neighbor, we love God in our neighbor. Similarly, q. 24, a. 1: "Therefore, it is clear that the act is essentially one and the same, when God is loved in the person of one's neighbor." Love is the holy unison that proceeds from God's Trinity like an eternal torch, setting the soul of man alight with a divine glow which spreads its warmth in all directions. It is the quality which, while straining toward God, yet sends its warm rays earthwards to diffuse all the daily details with love for one's neighbor. It is essentially this same *caritas* that lifts man to the blissful status of a child of God, that makes him long to immerse himself in mystical unity with all the profound majesty of the Godhead, and yet leaves him ready at any moment to turn toward his fellow man, yet, even to tear himself away from the divine embrace in order "to hand a little bowl of soup" to some poor beggar, his brother in Christ (Meister Eckhart). It is the kind of love that is not obliged to give, but delights in giving as a privilege; that is not conscious of conferring favors, but rather of receiving them; that does not count its good works and recite them for the benefit of others, but gives itself because it cannot do otherwise, just as a flower blooms to fulfill its own future, or a precious stone sparkles, or the sun warms with its bright rays. It is precisely this equality, not to say identity, of God's love and love of one's neighbor that constitutes the majesty of the divine commandment and gives the human virtue its ruling position. It is that which, on the one hand, serves as the identification mark of God's love, its certain outward proof, and thereby also acts as a safeguard against mystical extravagance; and, on the other hand, gives brotherly love its supernatural basis, its selfless motive, and that eternal, all-embracing quality which draws everything toward it.

There is a subtle differentiation which allows love of God to be classed as a primary virtue but relegates love of one's neighbor—at any rate in practice—to a position of equality, or even inferiority, in comparison with chastity. This involves a serious misplacement and misunderstanding of the very essence of the divine commandment of love. While, in the face of such clear and unmistakable direction, the theologian should really not permit himself to enter into fine distinctions and quibbles, he is in danger of missing the right path through the very best intentions. Like Goethe's Faust he finds himself

> On a burnt-up, barren heath
> Led astray by an evil spirit,
> And all around lie luscious, verdant meadows!

Certainly those champions of chastity who delight in calling it the Queen of Virtues can find biblical passages to bolster up their attitude. But these very quotations should serve as a warning because they invariably need artificial trimming, and sometimes even emptying of their original significance, in order to fit the case. The unjustifiable cutting of St. Paul's dictum (Eph. 5: 3-4) has been mentioned. In the same sense, Wisdom 4: 1 is unfortunately also often falsely applied. In the original text it is not "a chaste generation with glory" that is praised, but a "chaste procreation" which emerges clearly both from the words and the context.[2] The passage in Wisdom 7: 11: "Now all good things came to me with her," which Doss and his imitators rely upon to prove that all other virtues proceed from chastity, is an artful and unjustifiable accommodation, for the passage relates not to chastity but to wisdom; and if it is to be stretched at all, it might with much more propriety be applied to love as the first fruit of the Holy Ghost (Gal. 5: 22). The sense of the beatitude (Matt. 5: 8), "Blessed are the clean of heart for they shall see God," is also frequently contracted in order to cover, as is so often the custom nowadays, nothing more than sexual purity. The expression "pure of heart" (*mundo corde*) occurs frequently in the Holy Scriptures. It denotes the inner moral state of the soul, in contrast with outward, Levitical cleanliness. Wherever sexual purity is meant, that special application is clearly indicated, as in I Kings 21: 4, and in Tobias 3: 16. Apart from that, wherever the Scriptures mention "pure of heart," the significance is invariably "unstained, free from sin," as Proverbs 20: 9; Psalm 50: 11; Psalm 23: 4 explicitly show. The beatitude of our Lord seems expressly to hark back to the last-mentioned passage. And apart from this, our Lord Himself gives the best definition of all when, in discussing what can render the heart impure, He mentions in the same Gospel, Matthew 15: 19: "evil thoughts, murders, adulteries, fornications, thefts, false testimonies, blasphemies." Surely the precious virtue of chastity is sufficiently beautiful in its own right—it has no need to prink itself out with borrowed plumage. The Scriptures contain so many genuine passages worthily extolling its beauty that there is no need to bend and distort others to fit a pet belief. The examples of Joseph in Egypt and of Susanna and the Elders prove that, even in the Old Testament, chastity and genuine trueheartedness were highly esteemed. The New Testament values them even more highly, and the additional ideal of voluntary virginity is raised to hitherto unknown preeminence. The inspiring example of the immaculate Mother of God, and the deep friendship between Jesus and the virginal John set the ideal of chaste, renouncing love in the very foreground of the New Covenant. Millions of virginal souls, of both sexes, have since then based their dedicated lives on these examples, giving themselves up to active love in the seclusion of convents or to practical deeds of charity on the mission field, following "the Lamb withersoever he goeth" (Apoc. 14: 4). Passages in which our Lord speaks of voluntary abstention from marriage (Matt. 19: 12) and condemns the lustful look (Matt. 5: 28) belong to the same order, as also do the many warnings and examples in the apostolic epistles. There has never been any attempt to withhold from chastity the high esteem which is its due; in fact, far too many passages proving this are unduly neglected. But of course nowhere in the Holy Scriptures is this virtue wrenched out of its natural place within the framework of morality as a whole, or enthroned in that solitary grandeur which misused or biased quotations tend to force upon it.

The whole teaching of the early fathers of the Church, as well as that of eminent theologians right down the centuries, leaves no doubt whatever about the primacy of love. All of them have constantly underlined it. Of course, the early fathers extolled chastity as one of the ornaments of Christ's Church; Cyprian and Ambrose as well as Augustine composed veritable hymns in praise of this virtue. But they never raised it above all other virtues; that pre-eminence was reserved for love alone. By the same token, they never singled out unchastity as the greatest sin; that description was applied to a breach of the commandment of charity. Augustine speaks of loveless virginity as unfruitful virginity (*sterilis virginitas—Enarrat. in Ps.* 99. 13). Ambrose echoes the same thought when he remarks that a virgin attains nothing simply by her virginity, but only achieves merit when she makes it fruitful by charitable works. This author, in his book on virginity (*De virginitate*, i. 7. 34), expressly repudiates the Manichean pretensions which attempted to glorify virginity at the expense of marriage.

It is quite true that even in the primitive Church occasional voices were raised here and there, showing a special partiality to the virtue of chastity. This attempt to place the moral accent primarily on sexual behavior is very noticeable in the previously mentioned *Banquet* written by Methodius of Olympus. The work is one of the finest hymns of praise that have come down to us from early Christian times and its theme is chastity. Methodius praises virginity as "the noblest and most beautiful way of living," one which, he maintains, "might be taken as the only soil and blossom from which immortality could spring" (I. Speech of Marcella). He speaks of it as "the greatest and most blessed gift mankind could offer God, one which has absolutely no counterpart in value" (V. Speech of Thallura). In publishing these views to the world, Methodius undoubtedly represents those who give chastity precedence over all other virtues; but we must not forget, as L. Fend [3] quite correctly points out, that in this work the bishop was more rhetorical than theological, and that his mental outlook, despite his opposition later to Origen, was still greatly influenced by Neoplatonism which, through its dualistic convictions, tended to treat the body as an evil thing. It may be that for this very reason, despite its high artistic merits, the book came in for some sharp criticism even among contemporary readers, as Methodius himself tells us.[4]

So far as medieval times are concerned, it is unnecessary to cite all the apt passages that occur in the literature of that lively and highly interesting theological period. Although the marked Platonic influence which dominated many of the theological schools in days prior to St. Thomas Aquinas led to a strong bias in favor of spiritualism, which was not always favorable to full appreciation of the sacredness of marriage,[5] still, there was no fundamental difference of opinion concerning the particular point we have in mind; all the different schools and systems agreed that, in accordance with Christ's teaching, love came first. We can therefore confine ourselves to the two outstanding authorities of this period who are most often quoted—St. Bernard, because he is regarded as the chief exponent of the idea that unchastity is the greatest sin; and St. Thomas Aquinas, who is universally recognized as the supreme figure in medieval moral theology.

If we diligently search the writings of Bernard, we will find that the frequently quoted "extract"—"Pride is the sin of angels, greed the sin of man and unchastity that of beasts"—does not occur in any of them! It could, perhaps, be traced back to the famous court preacher, Bourdaloue, as we shall show further on. Hunolt appropriated it, and it was taken from him by his German imitators. It is ironical that, in dealing with sins of license, Bernard was always particularly moderate in tone, and he also took great care not to overrate the claims of virginity. His moral teaching differs from that of Thomas, which was to follow, chiefly in the particular stress he lays on humility, giving this a slight preference. Thomas, on the other hand, is slightly inclined to give justice the first place. In accordance with his predilection for humility, it is not surprising that St. Bernard refers again and again to pride as an offense the gravity and danger of which he never tires of stressing. But in his own fashion, the "honey-tongued teacher" [6] is fond of underlining the primacy of love. "Chastity without love is an oilless lamp. Take away the oil, and the lamp can no longer glow. Take away love, and chastity is no longer pleasing." [7] In praising virginity he deliberately puts it on a plane somewhat lower than humility, even with all his enthusiasm for the celibate state. "Virginity is a praiseworthy virtue, but an even more necessary attribute is humility. God looked with greater favor on the humility of His handmaiden than on her maidenhood." [8] In *Sermo IV in Nativitate*, c. 2, he compares the virtues humility, chastity, and justice, again giving humility first place: "Whoever leads an impure life, offends against his body; whoever uses violence sins against his neighbour, but he who puffs himself up, sins against God. The libertine harms himself, the violent man harms others, but he who gives himself up to pride dishonours God Himself." [9] In his treatise *De conversione ad clericos*, c. 5, he emphatically enumerates the vices of the spirit, mentioning pride and covetousness as graver and more dangerous than the sins of the flesh—more dangerous because the sinner himself is seldom or not at all aware of them in examining his own conscience. It will, therefore, be seen that Bernard in his teaching takes a line almost diametrically opposite to the one his modern, so-called "disciples" ascribe to him. With the following sentence, for instance, he surely refutes the contention that there are no mitigating conditions (*parvitas materiæ*) in the Sixth Commandment: "Even when the sin, through lack of control, may appear to be a venial one, the lack of control is in itself a fault."[10] In many other passages this great teacher expresses the thought that unchastity is more a matter of outward behavior, an offense against public honor, whereas sins of the spirit, like pride and avarice, far exceed it in gravity. Bernard should, therefore, be regarded as one of the chief witnesses against that bias which tends to limit the moral sphere to sexual problems. How lenient, for instance, is his judgment in his letter to the Countess de Blois (*Ep.* 300) concerning the youthful delinquencies of her son. "The false steps of youth . . . can be excused by the great ebb and flow of moods which characterize this time of life . . . one must handle him in a spirit of gentleness, using persuasion; that way one will achieve far more than with harsh treatment and scoldings which would merely harden him."

Thomas goes more deeply into the exact order of the various virtues. He, more than any other authority, substantiates the teaching of the primacy of love and sets it up in a scientific framework. The Angelic Doctor certainly cannot be suspected of holding the value of chastity in too little esteem. To the present day his moral teaching still holds good and has never been questioned on any essential point.

Aquinas sets up a kind of ladder of virtues. At the very top of this ladder we find the divine virtues; immediately beneath them is the queen or chorus leader, love (1-2, q. 66, a. 6: *Utrum caritas sit maxima inter virtutes theologicas*). Love is the queen of virtues, the *excellentissima virtutum* (2-2, q. 23, a. 6) which is of higher esteem than even hope or faith (*in ordine perfectionis*), even though, by the reckoning of time (*in ordine generationis*), faith comes before love (1-2, q. 62, a. 4). Without love, every other virtue is of no account (a. 7), so that actually love rounds out, gives substance to every other virtue and to that extent excels them (a. 8).

Among the divine virtues, which he divides up into *virtutes intellectuales* (virtues of reason) and *virtutes morales* (virtues which are moral in the narrower sense), Thomas includes all the moral virtues. Highest of all are the virtues of reason (*nobiliores,* 1-2, q. 66, a. 3) at the head of which stands wisdom (a. 5); and the most important in the second order of divine virtues is justice (a. 4), followed by courage; and then comes moderation, which expresses itself in the control of the natural appetites and the sexual instincts. St. Thomas decides the order of precedence of the various virtues by their objective importance. Justice affects a man's dealings not only in regard to himself, but also in regard to others; moderation, on the other hand, is concerned only with the more elementary desires for nourishment and the satisfaction of the senses.

In 2-2, q. 152, a. 5, he even raises the question whether virginity is the greatest of all virtues. This he answers with a decided negative. The divine virtues outweigh complete virginity because they represent the ultimate goal, whereas virginity is only a means to that end. "The end is always more valuable than the means, which only serve the end." But there are among moral achievements others which approach even more closely to the target than virginity does; for instance, martyrdom and the monastic vow. The martyr offers up his own life; the monk surrenders his own will, which is even more commendable than the renunciation of sensual desire in celibacy. The praise which the Holy Scriptures (Apoc. 14: 4) and the early fathers (notably Cyprian and Ambrose) lavish on virginity, Thomas explains, is only meant "within the frame of chastity" (*in genere castitatis*), since viriginity seems more sublime than the chastity of married people or widows and widowers, because it has a special magic in the eyes of mankind. Thus, according to the teaching of "the angel of the schools," virginity can neither subjectively nor objectively claim the highest place in the moral scale. Subjectively, it must fall behind faith, hope, and love because these are greater. This means that the highest moral attainments are not reserved for one particular class of people; they can only be reached by practicing all the divine virtues, and are therefore equally within reach of lay people (whether married or unmarried) and of those who have taken religious vows. Objectively also, virginity can claim no priority because it is excelled in merit by martyrdom and the taking of religious vows. Many fine works like, for instance, the otherwise profound and admirable study by J. Ries, "Kirche und Keuschheit," [11] which describes virginity as the *highest* moral development of the Christian ideal of life, have neither Thomas nor the majority of the Western fathers on their side in taking this view. Roman liturgy to all intents and purposes also gives martyrdom precedence over virginity, since it prescribes red for vestments on the feasts of martyred virgins (Agnes, Cecilia, Lucy, etc.), while the liturgy of the calced Carmelites—strongly influenced by Oriental ideas—gives preference to white.

It is obvious that the great teacher of the Church had taken up arms against currents of thought which even in those days had begun to confuse morality with the control of the sexual instinct, for he examines the question whether this mastery deserves preference at the expense of all the other virtues (2-2, q. 141, a. 8: *Utrum temperantia sit maxima virtutum*). This article is particularly relevant to our present purpose because in this, the great thinker analyzes very carefully all the grounds that might lead to chastity being proclaimed the queen of virtues. In this analysis, he throws penetrating light on the motives which are just as mistakenly pressing the claims of chastity at the present time.

Aquinas devotes this section to the tracing of three false conclusions which may lead to an overrating of asceticism in general and of sexual renunciation in particular.

The first is due to an excessive respect for outward decorum (*honestas*—honor). Here Thomas and Bernard meet on common ground. It stands to reason that chastity is important in regard to honor and decency and, for that reason, it is justly held in high esteem since it denotes a mastery over those instincts which man shares with the brute beasts. Man demonstrates his superiority and dominion over the whole of creation by proving that he is not blindly led by instinct but able, through the exercise of reason and free will, to master it. But these grounds are insufficient for the evaluation of a virtue. Thomas definitely agrees with the opinion of Gregory the Great (*Moralia* 33. 12) who said that "sins of the flesh were less grievous but more shameful" than sins of the spirit (1-2, q. 73). In comparison with other virtues, chastity has more of a negative value. Purity derives its chief attraction "from the shamefulness of its opposite," which reduces man to the level of animals; it has no inherent value of its own. Decency and decorum, the consideration of what is most seemly, are best served by moderation. The Latin words *decorum* and *honestum* are expressly used as the opposite of *malum*, that is to say, inwardly evil. The great theologian is obviously concerned here with a tendency to confuse moderation (that is to say, an excessive accent on chastity) with more important matters—the setting up of a human, temporal standard in opposition to the eternal, unchangeable standard of God. Highly prized as honor is—and Thomas was the last to deduct one iota from that esteem—it is still a thing entirely of this world. God does not measure man's actions by the mundane standards of honor and baseness, but by good and evil. What man considers honorable or shameful very often has little in common with that which is good or bad, sinful or holy in God's eyes. Some actions which God condemns can appear heroic in men's eyes—or vice versa. Honor, when all is said and done, is far more closely linked with passing modes of thought, with human customs, than with the supernatural values of good and evil. The expression and coordination of morality depends upon these two standards, and the danger arises from getting them mixed.

The second false conclusion against which Aquinas warns us is the tendency to sum up the value of an achievement by the difficulties encountered in gaining the mastery, and the amount of energy demanded by the struggle against opposing temptations. According to this argument, chastity really deserves first place among the virtues because it calls for the victory over the strongest of all appetites, the sexual instinct. But here St. Thomas raises the query whether mastery of the sexual instinct really does call for exceptional will power. He does not admit that there is any ground for attaching undue importance to this virtue. Its chief function is to keep order in the life of an individual, whereas bravery and, still more, justice embrace not only a man's individual well-being, but the good of the whole community and are therefore of far greater value. The importance of a virtue must be measured, not by the personal effort involved, but by its contribution to universal good.

Similarly, it is just as false to rate a virtue by quantitative measure. Human appetites are with us all the time; consequently, a man is far more often called upon to exercise moderation in eating and drinking, or in the control of his sexual instincts, than he is to show justice or bravery. And yet these spiritual virtues have far more bearing on the general good than the entirely personal matter of a man's control over his own sensual instincts.

Of course, one might raise the objection that it is not quite right to tie up chastity with other appetites under the general term moderation, because chastity has a broader social significance. Intimately linked with the mystery of birth and the survival of the race, the importance of chastity extends far beyond the individual to family, nation, state, and Church, unlike mere moderation in eating and drinking which only has a bearing on the community when it affects individual survival. All the same, the analysis of St. Thomas gets to the heart of the matter by exposing the fundamental mistake of making achievement the standard by which moral values can be judged. This is the pit into which modern champions of the primacy of chastity have fallen.

NOTES

1. *Zeitschrift für katholische Theologie* (1922), p. 441.
2. [The Confraternity version reads, "Better is childlessness with virtue"; Monsignor Knox read, "How fair a thing is the unwedded life that is nobly lived."—Ed.]
3. *Bibliothek der Kirchenväter,* 2 (Kempton, 1911), 111.
4. *The Discrimination of Food and the Young Cow Mentioned in Leviticus* 1.
5. Compare the very informative work of D. Lindner, *Der usus matrimonii* (Munich, 1929), pp. 19, 27, 52, etc.
6. St. Bernard was known as the *Doctor mellifluus.*

7. "Castitas sine caritate, lampas est sine oleo; subtrahe oleum, lampas non lucet; tolle caritatem, castitas non placet."—*De officiis episcoporum,* III, 9.

8. "Laudabilis virtus virginitas, sed magis necessaria humilitas . . . respexit humilitatem ancillæ suæ Deus potius quam virginitatem."

9. "Itaque qui fornicator, peccat in corpus suum; qui injuriosus est, in proximum; qui extollitur et inflatum, in Deum. Fornicator semetipsum dehonestat, injuriosus molestat proximum, elatus, quod in se est, Deum inhonorat."

10. "Nam etsi forsitan culpa propter incontinentiam venialis est, ipsa tamen tanta incontinentia turpis est."—*In Cantica sermo,* 59.

11. J. Ries, "Kirche und Keuschheit," *Katholische Lebenswerte* (Paderborn, 1931), p. 123.

CHAPTER 5

Love and Chastity in the Balance

THE breadth and penetration of the great medieval theologian's logic is a source of constant astonishment to anyone who examines the works of St. Thomas Aquinas with great care. Here was a man writing amid the comparatively uncomplicated conditions of the thirteenth century, when the authority of the Church was scarcely called into question by the public at large—yet in his examination of moral laws, St. Thomas constantly raises points which seem only to have become realized in our own times. Among those we could include the contention with which we concluded the foregoing chapter, namely, that chastity should, in practical religious instruction at least, take precedence over all other virtues because the whole of human morality is based upon it. Even if we admit that love of God, according to the Holy Scriptures, comes first, should not the emphasis be on chastity for all practical purposes? Surely, its champions maintain, chastity is the essential preliminary of all other virtues, and also the greatest testimonial of divine love. Whoever, for pure love of God, succeeds in mastering the most insistent of all appetites, the sexual instinct, gives proof of supreme moral energy. It requires immense will power to keep this most elementary of all instincts under control, and anyone who succeeds in this must have strength enough to develop all the other virtues because they entail far less temptation.

A. von Doss, an author of many juvenile books which formerly enjoyed a wide circulation and were much esteemed, is one of the chief advocates of this viewpoint. He even devoted one whole book to enlarging upon it, his ultimate aim being to prove that "all other virtues derive their value and their luster" from chastity. "All other virtues make chastity their starting point—it is that which illumines and shows the way" (p. 40). The importance of this author, and the high reputation his writings enjoy, compel us to take up this challenge, for Doss has many disciples and imitators. One well-known publication endorses the high valuation of chastity as follows: "Theoretically love is most important, but for all practical purposes chastity must dominate because the whole religious belief and inspiration of a great many people is bound up in this aspect of *caritas*. They do not stumble over the most important factor, but come to grief a long time before they reach it, over something which is less important." [1] Which effectively turns the less important factor into the most important one! Similarly, another publication of the same opinion makes the whole argument turn on the will power this virtue demands, and the evil consequences of the sin which results when the will power is unequal to demands made upon it. "The sexual instinct is without parallel, not only because of its constant presence and elementary force, but above all because of the far-reaching consequences in cases of catastrophe. If it were not for the irresistible driving force of sex and all that follows in its train—discord, corruption, hatred, murder, destruction of the health—often of more than one person, and even of unborn generations—denial of God and His Church, calculated wickedness and despair, to mention only a few samples from the almost limitless catalogue, the 'Primacy of Love' would be child's play, with only one other possible threat, through the seventh commandment."[2] Adherents of this view overlook the fact that it introduces a prohibited dualism into both morality and teaching—the dualism between theory and practice. According to this reasoning we should have two principal virtues, one for the moralists and one for pastoral theologians; one for the catechism, and another for practical application to the everyday affairs of life (because it is decisive in matters of faith and religious belief). This dualism is not removed, but rather aggravated, by suggesting (in order to give the thing a pseudo-theological foundation) that there are really two kinds of virtues—"constitutional" virtues headed by love, and "dispositional" virtues, among which chastity is "undoubtedly" supreme. Because Thomas points out that the *dignitas* (worthiness) of a virtue must not be measured by its difficulty, these disputants draw the hasty conclusion that Aquinas supports them in their view, namely, that theory and practice "are not obliged under all circumstances to agree."[3]

Since Thomas devoted no fewer than five articles (*Sum. Th.*, 1-2, q. 62, a. 4; 2. 66, a. 6; 2-2, q. 23, a. 6; q. 141, a. 8; q. 152, a. 5) expressly to proving that love is the most outstanding and important of all virtues, he should really be safe from quotation as authority for the exact opposite! But even on its own merits, an inconsequent differentiation between theory and practice in the sense described above cannot be too emphatically denounced.

Some theories, it is true, are so "up in the clouds" that they can have no possible influence on practical, everyday life. Actually, the very word "theory" nowadays has a somewhat unsympathetic, out-of-this-world flavor, as if it were something linked with remote book learning, too often belied by practice and thus having very little real application to the existence we are obliged to lead. But the exact opposite can also occur. There are cases where practice has gone far astray from inspired theory, standardizing all that is spiritual by mechanical mass production methods which lead it further and further from the right path grounded on sound principles. Here practice fails to square with theory and it must therefore be corrected, a process which is not invariably painless. Not every theory is nebulous, just as not every practice is really practical. As its name denotes, theory is the reflective "following through" of an idea; practice is action with a definite end in view. Theory indicates the goal; practice seeks the way whereby it may be reached. Theory examines fundamental principles to see if they will hold water; practice seeks out the methods that emerge. Where theory ceases to indicate the direction, practice loses itself and wastes its energy on unessential details. This is especially the case where theories rest on well-attested knowledge and are therefore quite free from suspicion of being "nebulous." Here every contradictory practice, however well-meant it may be, is bound to go wrong from the very start. Moral theology establishes the principles; pastoral theology points the way in which these can best be realized. If pastoral and moral theology follow the rule of theory and practice, they cannot possibly get out of step. Pastoral theology is never justified in setting aside anything that moral theology establishes as the cornerstone of morality. If it does so, it is on the wrong road from the outset.

Luckily for us, we Catholics have the great good fortune to be spared dispute over essential theories. Our faith gives us sound principles, and our only task is to apply them to our lives. If mistakes were ever made in the Church, these never came about through any flaw in theory; they were caused by failure to apply the infallible principles which should control practical life. Few truths are mentioned so often, so emphatically, and so unmistakably in the Scriptures as the predominance of love over all other virtues; nor is any other truth repeated in so self-evident a fashion throughout theology as a whole. Both science and the educational authority of the Church have never hesitated to emphasize this truth as *the* dogma, the foundation of all Christian morality. No Catholic would dream of casting any doubt upon it; but of what use is all this intellectual conformity if, in his practical daily life, his normal actions, he substitutes something quite different for this fundamental truth? If, by pedantry, an attempt is made to juggle with the dogma in order to make it square with some other idea, this attempt, well-meant as it may be, is bound to be fruitless, for human wisdom can never take the place of the divine. This sort of thing turns sound morals into sterile "morality." It turns the conscientious into overscrupulous busybodies, and the lukewarm into Pharisees. One can say this without reflecting on the honest work and the serving the best ends by supporting this theory. But if men like Hunolt and Doss reached great achievements in their own day, the credit must be ascribed to their selfless labors, not to their mistaken methods. Despite all they preached, giving pre-eminence to chastity, it was really love that filled their lives like a warm, radiant sun dispensing its blessings through all their energies, much as they might theoretically and unconsciously deny this. It merely proves the old saying that a good teacher may achieve more by a false method than a bad teacher with a first-class system.

The very readiness with which, in contradiction to Thomas, chastity is repeatedly cited as the "Queen of Virtues" since it calls for exceptional will power, shows how much we have grown accustomed, by insidious stages, to linking up morality with strength of will. It is easy to recognize in this the influence of a theological system which came into prominence following the Council of Trent. Because it gave particular emphasis to the doctrine of the freedom of will, which the Reformation movement severely threatened at that time, it seemed the best answer to the *sola fides* teaching of the Reformers who claimed to rely upon faith alone, and this gave it the ascendancy it gradually established in Catholic circles. Molinism—or congruism, as it was called after Bellarmine and Suárez had improved the original system—employed moral and religious energies with powerful effect during the period of the Counter Reformation and did a great deal of good. The system in no way disputes the influence of grace and for that reason it is recognized by the Church, even though long, wordy battles were fought in the so-called "quarrel" over the question of divine grace. But no theological system invented by man represents the faith of the Church as a whole, and that is why the educational authority of the Church has never identified itself with any particular school or system. Each school of thought has its own individual quality and runs the risk of overstepping the mark if some of its representatives, more enthusiastic than wise, accentuate that quality unduly and thus tend to upset the harmonious structure of faith, which would certainly happen if other schools and systems did not keep the scales of Catholic public opinion evenly balanced.

Naturally, it would never occur to a Catholic preacher to alter an article of the Catholic faith or consciously to obscure its sense. And with all its emphasis on freedom of will, Molinism never denied that the decisive factor in the Christian's moral endeavor was grace, not will. Nevertheless, superficial theological thinking can far too easily run the risk of missing the fine demarcation line which separates Molinism, the Catholic system of grace, from Semi-Pelagian error. This danger is all the greater when rhetoric or even polemics, rather than theology, are the actuating motive of the argument. Will power always makes a stronger appeal than the need for supernatural grace, which will never cease to be a mystery to human reason. There was a time—not so long ago—when personal "will control" occupied the mental picture so completely as to leave no room whatever for supernatural grace in moral life. Grace was looked upon as a mere appendage, an aid which God extended to wrestling, struggling mankind—it was no longer *the* life, the very air of inspiration and respiration without which we should be incapable of even the effort of mortal striving. People no longer spoke of sanctifying grace; they preferred to call it helpful grace. This did not amount to a denial of supernatural grace—it simply meant that, for the regulation of a practical Christian life, the correct conclusions had not been drawn. Even where the need for supernatural grace, and its all-powerful quality, were dutifully explained, there was a quite involuntary tendency to convey the impression that everyone's individual quota of grace could be earned by diligent prayer and eagerness to receive the sacraments. Thus, by implication, supernatural grace depended indirectly on the exercise of the human will. The moral status of a community was measured by its confessional and communion statistics. An abundance of devotions, practices, and projects lent color to the conviction that the final decision rested with the human will. Through all this, the ground was well prepared for the reception of an idea which Aquinas had centuries before proved to be demonstrably wrong, namely, that the power of the will, as proved by the mastery over the strongest of all instincts, gave chastity priority over all other virtues. It may have struck the observant reader that all the chief representatives of this viewpoint belong to the Molinistic school. Molinism does not necessarily lead to it—this is far more a case of biased emphasis which leads overzealous adherents to stretch certain fundamental ideas out of true proportion. Every idea, no matter how true it may be, can lead to exaggeration and error if accepted beyond its natural meaning. Unless it is balanced by Thomistic counterpoise, Molinism runs the risk of overstepping the border line in the direction of free will. Thus, practically if not theoretically misguided pedagogic considerations may make will power the most important goal of moral endeavor. This is an error which, even in the early days of the Church, many sincere and holy men fell into. Typical examples are John Cassian (d. 435) who deserves the utmost esteem for his wisdom and asceticism; the learned Vincent of Lérins (d. about 450); and the holy Faustus of Riez (d. *c.* 493). All of these, through their fear that emphasis placed too exclusively on supernatural grace might weaken human will power, fell into the error of Semi-Pelagianism. No doubt Augustine, the greatest advocate of the Catholic doctrine of divine grace, would shake his head over a good many sermons which are being preached today on the virtue of chastity and the grace of constancy!

The moral heights a man can reach are not determined primarily by his strength of will, but by the power of divine grace which, though man's cooperation is entirely necessary, yet altogether outweighs it. If a man succeeds in overcoming temptation, even that is primarily due to divine grace, as the Council of Orange (529), confirmed by Pope Boniface II, in its decision against the Semi-Pelagians, testifies: "If anyone says divine grace can be obtained by appealing for it, and not that it is divine grace itself that moves us to call upon God, he contradicts the prophet Isaias, and the Apostle, who says: 'But Isaias is bold and saith, I was found by them that did not seek me. I appeared openly to them that asked not after me' " (Isai. 65: 1; Rom. 10: 20; DB 176). "If anyone maintains that God awaits our will, to cleanse us from sin, but that this will does not arise through yielding to the prompting of the Holy Ghost within us, he resists the same Holy Ghost, which is made clear by the sermon of the Apostle: 'For it is God who worketh in you, both to will and to accomplish, according to His good will' " (Phil. 2: 13; DB 177).[4] The same council lays great stress on the fact that man's moral attainments are due to divine grace and not to any effort of his own will. This is especially brought out by canons 6, 9, 11 (DB 179, 182, 184). Canon 12 (DB 185) expressly states that His divine grace is due to His love for us, and is not in any way a reward for our own merit.[5]

All these clear, dogmatic decisions prove how false it is to measure a virtue by the effort involved in practicing it, and how little the habit of giving chastity the ascendancy over all other virtues, on this ground alone, is justified. Much of our recent literature cannot escape the reproach of departing on this point from the solid basis of sound theology, or at least of denying in practice what is still theoretically the substance of Christian moral teaching, and will always remain so.

If the main part of this statement, namely, that the value of a virtue cannot be measured by the moral energy it entails, is false, then its subsidiary clause, that chastity is the most difficult of virtues, lies equally open to question.

Which virtue requires more self-control and strength of will, chastity or love? The answer will doubtless depend on the temperament and inclination of the person questioned. Many a hot-blooded man has to exert supreme effort to control himself in sexual matters, and encounters greater difficulties than others. It may easily appear to a pliant nature that it is easier to forgive an insult than to overcome unchaste desires. But it is surely unjustifiable to generalize on such a question and to declare out-of-hand that the mystery of sexual instincts calls for greater will power than the exercise of love. The claims of love are far more demanding and numerous than the demands of chastity, and they call for an enormous amount of daily detail work—sometimes, indeed, also for heroic self-sacrifice. The heroism of love by no means falls short of the heroism of chastity; in fact, it is usually the other way about. And we need not even fall back on heroic examples like Elizabeth of Hungary and Damian the Leper. No, it is just as palpable in everyday occurrences, as, for instance, where poverty is rampant and the last crust is cheerfully shared with others; or where an uneasy yoke of matrimony is borne with silent patience, or where open hostility is met with forgiving meekness. Very few people are called upon to demonstrate love by noble deeds or unique achievements. It is renunciation of one's own beloved ego, an enduring, selfless way of everyday living. Control of one's own emotions, forbearance when other people's moods offend, invariable kindness toward those we have to live with, despite all their whims and idiosyncrasies; conscientious performance of our duty in gaining our means of livelihood—despite any annoyance our fellow-workers may cause us—are no less important than guarding against hasty judgments and prejudices, against outbreaks of temper and impatience, against giving way to nervous storms. All these things, together with a willingness to allow other people their own point of view, and a recognition of the right moment to speak or to remain silent, call for a measure of will power which is not often to be found among those who need all the moral energy they can muster to keep a guard on their erotic impulses. Whoever, after a daily examination of conscience, is not obliged to sigh a *mea culpa* for some trespass in these respects must be either a saint or a hypocrite. There are Christians, it is true, who regard as comparatively venial those offenses affecting the love of God or their neighbors, while they find their consciences unduly troubled by the least sexual urge, even if it is involuntary; but the very fact that this is so surely argues a mistaken pedagogic method which inclines to abnormal preoccupation with sexual matters and neglects all the other moral obligations. Daily denial of the personal "I" in the service of love is an achievement that excels exceptional feats of self-mortification and asceticism—one which our Lord Himself has recommended in the words: "If any man will come after me, let him deny himself and take up his cross daily and follow me" (Luke 9: 23). "Love of man for man is perhaps the most difficult task that has been laid upon us, the ultimate, final test, the one undertaking that renders all other labor a mere preliminary preparation for it."—Rainer Maria Rilke.

There is just one other elementary human urge which, for irresistible force, can compare with the sexual instinct, and that is selfishness. One might argue ad infinitum as to which of the two is more imperative. Certainly the sexual urge is a primitive force, but egoism in the long run can tyrannize in ways which even surpass the tyranny of sex. The contention, "The enduring strength of the sexual urge in the subject is without parallel,"[6] proves untenable because human egoism certainly outbids it in this respect. Eroticism is not always manifest to the same degree in all normal people. There are times when it remains dormant; and at other times, as in old age, it ceases completely. But egoism, from earliest youth to dotage, is always present and always at work, subjecting every thought, word, and deed to its penetrating poison. If Eros can be likened to an occasional flood tide which, under certain circumstances, will bring great destruction in its wake, the personal "I," on the other hand, is like an ever-present river, leaving its deposits of slime and refuse incessantly on the banks. Moreover, egoism is far more difficult to recognize and to combat because it loves to hide under attractive disguises, like love, honor, efficiency and service, enthusiasm for God, patriotism, and what not. There is nothing an egoist will not make use of in an attempt to cover up his self-seeking motives. The most brutal indifference to other people's rights will pass itself off as energetic efficiency; disparagement wears the cloak of pharisaical moral rectitude, relentlessness masquerades as justice, greed as frugality, while hate and revenge pose as zeal for religion or the state. The man who is tempted to transgress against chastity is not nearly in as great or as enduring a danger as the man who has to deal with the constant importunity of his own self-love.

For the same reason, it is a false procedure to estimate the gravity of a sin by its danger and draw conclusions from the distinction—as if the sin which most contradicts the known will of Almighty God could at the same time be anything but the most dangerous confronting mankind. Some admit that sins against the commandment of love are certainly the most grievous—but simultaneously contend that sins against chastity are the most dangerous and must, therefore, be singled out for special emphasis in practical religious teaching. This kind of logic not only commits the error already mentioned, of putting practice and sound theory in opposition to each other; it also overlooks the well-known fact that the most dangerous sins are the ones that look quite innocent and therefore deceive the conscience. It is true that the violence of the erotic urge often exceeds that of all other elementary instincts. In the interests of the survival of the species, Almighty God has seen fit to make the sexual urge almost irresistible in order that it may cancel out the restricting motives that spring from consciousness of responsibility and the labor involved in carrying on the race; thus, man is forced into the service of the race involuntarily and against his own ease and convenience. To this extent the sexual instinct can be a real danger to the man lacking in self-control. All the same, sins against the commandment of love for God and one's neighbor are infinitely greater and of more far-reaching detriment on moral grounds, since these are like a sly enemy masking evil designs under a mantle of friendship. With an open enemy, one knows where one stands. Furthermore, by making this distinction, we are flattering ourselves that our own human observation and experience are quite worthy to be set above the clear truth as revealed to us in God's own commandment. Whether we like it or not, God did actually pronounce love—and not chastity—to be the greatest of all commandments. So why should we resort to all kinds of human distinctions and reflections instead of accepting the clear and unmistakable word of God, and making it the guiding principle of our lives and our practical religious instruction?

Even the sexual sins arrive at their full measure of iniquity only insofar as they offend against the commandment of love. When two young people in the full glow of passion forget the commandment, the trespass only becomes tragic and its consequences evil if one of the offenders has exploited that passion for self-seeking satisfaction without any intention of meeting the responsibilities involved. Every sin attains its actual evil only through the absence of love which it demonstrates, just as it is the presence of love in every good deed that gives it the warm glow of holy fire. This also explains why in the lives and legends of great saints we so often come across men and women who in their youth had paid tribute to the lure of the flesh—but we very rarely, if ever, come across a converted egoist. A Mary Magdalene was deemed worthy to be in the closest proximity to Jesus; Augustine, despite his youthful follies, stands in the very forefront of the Church's fathers; a St. Afra who, in Augsburg, performed the shameful duties of a temple prostitute, is yet revered as one of the earliest saints. The history of the saints contains details of many such conversions—I. F. Coudenhove-Görres observes that we have among the saints "past lives" of every kind, but, so far as her observation goes, not one of the cold, avaricious type.[7] The hard miser; the ruthless place-seeker; the calculating, immoral business man; the narrow-minded faultfinder; the envious, backbiting rival—all these egoists are more objectionable types than the man of weak resistance battling bravely with his passionate disposition.

On the other hand, the inference that a man who is able to master his sexual impulses stands a better chance of excelling in all other virtues is contradicted by everyday observation. We all know from our own experience that there are many people who lead a perfectly "moral" life, yet are completely unequal to the will power required to control their own moods. *Castitas sine caritate*, chastity without love, of which Bernard speaks, is far more common than its opposite, love without chastity. Where the Holy Scriptures speak in glowing terms of untarnished purity, describing it as so pleasing to God that it is "sung as it were a new canticle" (Apoc. 14: 3), this distinction only applies to chastity when it is bound up with love and humility. Where these are lacking, chastity becomes a repellent, proud, puritanical, or pharisaical quality; the kind of bearing that strides arrogantly into the very front part of the temple and stands there looking with contempt on the poor publican in the shadows. The sex-ridden individual is more likely to be humble, loving, and meek; therefore, despite many weaknesses, he is often of greater moral stature than one who, for no physical reason, is virginal, but lacks the oil of love. "But to whom less is forgiven, he loveth less" (Luke 7: 47). Although chastity may be subject to very severe temptations in times of passion, and may sometimes have to withstand the most painful tests, it can yet call to its aid many natural protections, such as a sense of shame, an inner feeling for purity, and the outward armor of honor and a good name. Many a person hardly touched by religious considerations will, in this connection, exercise caution on conventional grounds, fearing loss of reputation or the hygienic consequences which may follow an unfortunate lapse. These are completely human motives which the virtue of love certainly cannot press into service, and they should be remembered when weighing up the respective merits of love and chastity.

To regard chastity, because of its inherent demands on will power, as the kernel of all practical morality, the *punctum puncti,* "the beacon which lights the way for all virtues" and therefore deserves to be called their Queen, is pointless and dangerous. It is not in accordance with scriptural authority and in fact it completely contradicts the divine command. Nowhere does the Bible refer to chastity as the foundation on which all virtues are based; but it very often speaks of them as being the consequence of love. "Owe no man anything but to love one another. For he that loveth his neighbor hath fulfilled the law" (Rom. 13: 8). Of all the great teachers of the Church, it is Thomas Aquinas who follows through this thought with the deepest penetration. He calls love the root, the basis, the mother of all other virtues (*Sum. Th.,* 1-2, q. 62, a. 4; 2-2, q. 23, a. 7 & 8, etc.). "He who has love possesses all other virtues." "No true virtue can exist without love" (1-2, q. 65, a. 3). He therefore designates love *forma virtutum*—"the form out of which all other virtues are sustained and nourished" (2-2, q. 23, a. 7 & 8) and gives, as the reason for this: "because, through love, the activities of all the other virtues derive their direction and ultimate goal." In that respect, it is permissible to describe love as the constitutional principle of morality. But it is also the greatest among the dispositional virtues, if one can make this differentiation here. It is not only the sun which warms and illuminates the whole of moral life from within, but it is also that which gives all the other virtues their motive and aim, endorsing them inwardly and outwardly, especially in actions that affect brotherly love. Our Saviour repeatedly refers to outward and visible signs of God's love within and, as their living proof, He nowhere mentions any virtue other than brotherly love. "By this shall all men know that you are my disciples if you have love one for another" (John 13: 35). The Apostle of Love delights in dwelling upon this thought: "If any man say: I love God, and hateth his brother, he is a liar" (I John 4:20). "And this commandment we have from God, that he who loveth God loveth also his brother" (I John 4:21). The second and third chapters of the First Epistle of St. John are devoted almost entirely to proving that the surest outward sign of divine love is to be found in love of one's neighbor. "He that hath the substance of this world and shall see his brother in need and shall shut up his bowels from him: how doth the charity of God abide in him?" (I John 3: 17).

In the face of such clear dogmatic facts, one ought to beware of dragging artificial distinctions and the deceptive conclusions of obscure dualism into morality—the kind of distinction that recognizes love theoretically as the chief virtue, but in practice makes chastity the axis on which all moral dealings revolve. The consequences of such teaching are bound to produce a marked shifting accent by making a side issue, however important it may be in its own right, the focal point of morality. This is bound to have a detrimental effect upon the whole of practical religious teaching because it dissipates the instructor's energies and often withdraws his strength from the main point of attack in order that he may defend a bastion which is comparatively less important.

The chief cause of this shifting of accent, as already explained, can be traced even in Catholic circles to a moral outlook which is not substantiated by the Holy Scriptures but has its roots in Platonic philosophy. Oriental Manicheism is essentially foreign to Western thought, and it would never have become a serious menace had it not appropriated many of the elements of Plato's noble philosophy. The error which most crudely opposes truth is not always the most dangerous. Such danger arises much more insidiously from errors which lurk like poison among the golden grains of valuable knowledge. Catholic thought has always repudiated Manicheism, but the idea of pure spirituality has always had a strong attraction for deeply religious souls. Like a scarlet thread it runs through the whole of the history of Catholic mysticism from Origen onwards through the early fathers of the Church who came under his influence; and it has more than once forced the Church to step in with firm decisions. The moral theologian, D. Lindner of Freising, in his excellent little book, *Der Usus matrimonii,* has clearly shown how greatly the Neoplatonic teaching of spirituality has influenced the greater majority of Catholic theologians and to some extent hindered them in an objective appraisal of sexual facts. The history of marriage morality is the story of an almost continual conflict inside theology—a fight against opinions which, in the name of so-called "higher" morality, tended to depreciate marriage. They are to be found even among great thinkers like Origen and Jerome; [8] the earlier writings of Augustine contain traces of them, too, as do those of other learned men before the time of Thomas Aquinas. To the Platonist, all appetite was in any case suspect, as being unspiritual, and suppressed as much as possible. Therefore, the Platonist was disinclined to favor marriage and he took the sternest possible view of its consummation. When Aristotelian reasoning emerged, with Albertus Magnus and Thomas, the basic question whether lust in a good action is good,[9] just as, in an evil action, it is bad, naturally arose and claimed a good deal of attention. An unprejudiced weighing up of the lust-principle might have paved the way to a more just evaluation of marriage. But even then there were theologians who contended that sexual lust should be excluded from the basic question as being quite special, even in the sphere of the senses, since its violence could rise superior to spirit. And so it happened that many, even among Aristotelian thinkers, joined with those who supported the former belief that consummation of marriage was impossible without committing venial sin—they scarcely dared to call it mortal sin out of respect for the sacrament of marriage and the definite ruling of the Church. Consummation of marriage was only admitted as being guiltless when it took place solely for the procreation of children. The fact that for centuries the only writers to deal with marriage and marriage morals were celibates, who may from the outset have tended to bring little sympathy to bear on the positive qualities of mutual love and the intimate comradeship of married people, doubtless took its own revenge. Not until the eighteenth century were the Jesuits and the Carmelites of the University of Salamanca gradually able to overcome this mistrust—not without great opposition from Manichean and puritanically-inclined Jansenist influences. Nowadays, Catholic marriage morality, in which the views of married lay people, doctors, philosophers, and also women are well represented, brings a broader understanding to bear on the "love relationship in marriage, the seeking-and-finding of self as designed and divinely ordained by the Creator."[10] If here and there in some writings the unjustifiable words *partes inhonestæ*,[11] as applied to the sex organs, still appear, or the concepts of "passion" and "sensuality" are only treated in a condemnatory sense, this may be attributed to inexact phraseology rather than to Manichean thinking. But the present state of affairs forces us to exercise extra care in the way we express ourselves, and we have to keep very scrupulously to the original meaning of words lest we should bring grist to the mills of many young Nietzsches who are only too eager to seize upon this kind of slovenliness to prove their charge of Manicheism and stress the so-called "enmity toward Nature," of which they are constantly accusing the Church.

Of course, as F. Walter [12] has pointed out, we should not forget that there are still very active factors in the Christian world which can be taken to indicate disdain or, at any rate, to look askance at all things physical—that is to say, unless we look at them in proper focus, as integral parts of the teachings as a whole.

The *unum necessarium,* of which our Lord Himself spoke as the one thing necessary for the attainment of eternal salvation (Luke 10: 42), demands that a Christian shall under certain circumstances renounce earthly ease and pleasure for the sake of a heavenly reward. Thoughts of death and the transient nature of all temporal things, of which the Scriptures constantly remind us, will permit no Christian to give himself up completely to this life on earth, with its burdens and its ecstasies, its recurrence of long, humdrum weeks and occasional feast days. The Christian religion, centered round the Crucified One, the Man of Sorrows, puts a certain reserve on enthusiasm for all the lures and joys of the world and all the compensations the senses have to offer. The dogma of original sin teaches us to distrust the world's glamour, with its pride, its distractions, its enticing outward beauty. It also offers us a contrasting picture of the world—this vale of tears, full of pitfalls for the unwary soul.

No one can deny that such warnings do actually receive prominence in the teachings of the Church and that they make an imperative appeal to earnest Christians. We who believe have no quarrel with them; we accept them gladly. But it must not be forgotten that these truths do not represent the whole of Christianity. They are only parts that require amplification in order to be properly appreciated. Not until they are seen in their right context, harmoniously woven into the whole fabric of the faith, do they attain their full meaning. It may well be that a Lenten sermon, or a mission address, tends to lay particular emphasis on this, that, or the other truth, in order to jolt us to attention. Actually, however, these amount to no more than a sober statement of facts which any ordinary person can recognize even without revelation, or of requirements of conduct that Christianity shares with the teachings of all right-minded men throughout the ages. In this connection, Goethe's thoughts come to our mind. This great writer said: "Indulgence vulgarizes." Ang again: "Die . . . . in order that you may *become*." Purely pedagogic considerations may tempt some teachers to lay undue stress on the more serious truths of Christianity, thereby overshadowing, to some extent, the lighter and happier aspects of revealed truth which our Lord Himself described as "tidings of great joy." But the whole history of Christ's Church, with two thousand years of culture behind it, proves that, far from being a kill-joy, the Church ardently fosters happiness, true beauty, and love. Since, in agreement with St. Paul, the body is recognized as the temple of the Holy Ghost, and since prominence is given to man's being created "in the image and likeness of God" on the very first page of the Bible, the Christian attitude to the human body in no way falls short of the lofty pretensions which the modern apostles of beauty culture, physical fitness, and sensuality have thought up. If the religion of the Cross keeps before man's eyes the dangers of materialism, thus enabling him to recognize the insidious poison of a hedonic pandering to the senses, it is supporting the claims of physical culture far more than the much-vaunted maxims of Epicurus and his teaching and example. The Church does uphold a standard which is of infinitely greater service to the sanctity of marriage, the well-being of the family, to love, to loyalty, and to the health of the race as a whole, than are the Dionysian teachings of modern "reformers" who, by stressing the claims of the senses, are robbing youth of all ideals and of that very resistance which makes good the contention that the sexual instinct is all-powerful and irresistible.

But, in his polemic handling of the moral Christian approach to materialistic lusts, the preacher should avoid the temptation to exaggerate. That would be setting up Beelzebub in place of the devil. The need for clear-cut logic is greater today than it has ever been, and it is equally necessary not to cover up the Christian assessment of the physical and sensual with a tactical spirituality which is not based on biblical authority. Our Lord, who spoke of "the one thing necessary" (Luke 10: 42), never once hinted at a Manichean disdain of the body in His commandments and recommendations. In fact, He expressly refrained from requiring of His disciples the fasting and the severe ascetic practices, the total renunciation of joy, which in those days were looked upon as self-evident accompaniments of a sincere striving for religious perfection. His own delight in nature is only too obvious. Think of the examples He quotes—the lilies of the field, the birds of the air, seeds germinating in the soil, lambs disporting themselves in the meadows. With such lovely verbal material He chooses to clothe the eternal truths. He participates in the marriage feast at Cana and in Simon's banquet; He enjoys the artless play of children and takes the keenest interest in the way fishermen, farmers, shepherds, servants, and merchants live. He knows all about the struggles of the poor widow and the spendthrift prodigality of the rich man's son. There is absolutely no cramping narrowness about Him; He is completely natural—so much so that His opponents find fault with the very simplicity, the lack of pomp about this Messias who calls Himself the Son of God. Although He holds up for admiration the ideal of celibacy "for the kingdom's sake," He never disparages marriage. Again and again He shows a preference for using the wedding feast as an apt illustration for the Kingdom of God, and it is He who restored the conception of marriage itself to its original purity, unity, and mutual trust.

The teaching on Original Sin is equally far removed from what has been called "enmity to nature." Those who make this charge on the ground of Manichean tendencies inside the Church are ignorant of the fact that this calumny is without foundation, because what they believe to be the Catholic attitude toward Original Sin is actually the teaching of the Reformers, and has been unequivocally repudiated by the Church. This truth, also, is only a part of the whole picture; it is merely the first page of another bright, joyous truth: that of salvation. That is why the liturgy of the Church is bold enough to use, for Holy Saturday, the apparent contradiction "*felix culpa,*" "the happy sin, which has earned for us so great a Redeemer." Certainly the world comes under the curse of sin; but, through the Redemption, that which was meant for punishment has been transformed into a means of triumph. Christian preachers who keep their eyes too exclusively fixed on Original Sin, thus encouraging a pessimism based on preoccupation with guilt and temporal matters, are in the wrong. Even in our own camp, it is sometimes overlooked that the concept of the world is used in the Scriptures in a double sense. It can trip a man up because of its own imperfection and man's sinful inclinations. It is in this sense that our Lord warns us against the world; and the Apostle says: "Love not the world, nor the things which are of the world" (I John 2: 15). But the world is also God's divine creation, and of this creation the Scriptures remark, after each day's accomplishment, this came from the hand of the Lord, and was good. In this sense the same Apostle tells us, "God so loved the world as to give His only-begotten Son" to save the world. The Psalmist invites all creation to glorify God in it. It is precisely the believing Christian who can enjoy the world, recognizing his brother or sister in every human being, and God in every creature, plant and flower, as St. Francis of Assisi did; for all, like himself, are divinely created so that they may praise God and, by their very existence, please Him.

The senses as well as the spirit belong to this created world. In the light of true faith, the body and sex are not merely tolerated as if they were things we should really be better without. They are not unclean, despicable, but God-created in accordance with His divine will and blessed by His divine grace. Starting from this fact, the Christian is bound to arrive at a positive evaluation of sex, as the faithful in earliest Christian times and in the Middle Ages have demonstrated. Eros is not merely a demoniac power who creates chaos and destruction, locking the whole of life in binding fetters. In all ages, this same power has been a source of irresistible energy. The love of man and woman, which God has placed in the heart of mankind as one of the mightiest aids to the maintenance of the species, is also one of the greatest inspirations of human culture. This is the force which sets heroism aflame and inspires artists; it urges men on to achievements which they would never dream of attempting in their sober senses. Where would the divine spark of poetry be, or the sweet harmony of our composers, not to mention the deep feeling which moves us to much in the old folk songs, but for this inner urge which can turn any stripling into a poet? All the great creative artists mankind has produced were sensitive, not to say sensual, individuals; and we should bring a sympathetic understanding to bear upon their failings if now and then they overstepped the bounds, not only of narrow convention, but even of the accepted moral code. "Only the mettlesome thoroughbred precipitates itself pluckily onto the racecourse; the donkey steps out at a thoughtful pace" (Schiller). Can we not detect a note of this same tolerance in the words of our Lord: "But to whom less is forgiven, he loveth less" (Luke 7: 47)? Masculine strength, feminine charm, masculine will, feminine nature; masculine enterprise, feminine eagerness to serve—where would the world be without these apparent opposites which yet amplify and complete each other and represent the perpetual interplay of body and soul, of the physical and the spiritual, of Amor and Psyche? With the dawn of this contrast, the spiritual urge for achievement awakens, taking the form of youthful idealism and a trend toward art, poetry, honor and valor. Certainly the natural Eros is capable of anything—of noble deeds or of abysmal follies, of highest self-sacrifice or senseless destruction. But does this entitle us to condemn the intensity of the fire which can cook a meal or bake a potter's masterpiece and, on the other hand, is also capable of burning down an entire city, sweeping away countless works of art in its destructive course? Man tries by every art to harness destructive forces and employ them constructively for his own convenience and profit. It is equally morality's task to use the mighty power of this primitive urge to the highest ends, but no part of true morality's function either to malign or condemn the sexual instinct.

This task of taming, cleansing, and healing the sexual instinct falls on *caritas*. *Sexus-Eros-Caritas*—these are the three stages of purely sensual, spiritual, and divine love. One of them does not look down upon the other; each proceeds to build on that which preceded it.[13] Lust and love meet in Eros, the sensual and the spiritual closely linked, filled with indulgence and laden with energy. But *caritas* is the baptized Eros, able even to augment the urge of natural love because of the strength from supernatural grace. All the moral energies we call virtues spring from this: justice, valor, truthfulness, humility. Most of all, however, *caritas* loves to join with chastity. In this most binding alliance, love is stronger than death. Together they hasten, fleet of foot, across oceans and wildernesses, bringing the gospel of love to places where there is no light; together they watch through long, weary nights by beds of sickness. This is the love that will share its last crust with a hungry child; that offers itself in atonement before the tabernacle of that divine love that condescended to be made man and dwell among us. Love and chastity—where these two are joined, thorns blossom and deserts turn green; miracles occur which astonish the angels and glorify God. But the greatest of them all is the miracle of love.

Love is not more precious because it is chaste; but chastity is precious only when it is the embodiment of love. The mere renunciation of the sexual function has no inherent merit; whoever ascribes any merit to it arrives logically at the ideal of perfection a Manichean or an Indian fakir has in mind. Renunciation of marriage does not achieve its true value until it is sanctified by selfless love. Christ our Lord distinguishes three different kinds of celibacy—the first through natural incapacity "from the mother's womb," the second caused with or without a person's will, and the third "for the kingdom of heaven's sake" (Matt. 19: 12): that is to say, in the service of the kingdom of God. There is a fourth which springs from disdain of marriage, and a fifth which springs from pure convenience, but our Lord does not mention these. Anyone who renounces marriage from a sense of duty—apart from involuntary incapacity or the use of force—is only justified in this renunciation if something equally valuable is given for the kingdom of God in exchange for that which failure to marry denies. Celibacy does not mean the renunciation of love but on the contrary increases it, broadens it beyond the range of family till it reaches to the farthest limits of God's kingdom. We all know the creative urge that stimulates artistic genius; the unselfishness of the soldier who sacrifices his life for his country; the single-mindedness of learned men who give up their whole life to research; the divine flame that glows in the heart of the poorest mother when she yearns over her child. It is that same grace, pulsating with supernatural strength, that moves idealistic souls to relinquish all thought of family and a home of their own because so many tasks in the kingdom of God—tasks in which the fetters of family would be a hindrance—claim their undivided love. Orphans who need an adoptive mother will always be with us; there will always be poor people who hunger not only for bread but still more for sympathetic love; there will always be the sick who require not only a helping hand but also tender, healing care. There will also always be married couples who need a good example of self-control and renunciation. Side by side with physical life there will always be values of a more spiritual, a moral kind, which are even more important to the community—life forces which need to be passed on by those to whom spiritual relationship means more than blood brotherhood; those who desire to do the will of the Father who is in heaven, that he might become Christ's brother or sister or mother (cf. Matt. 12:50). Anyone who refrains from entering the married state for any other reason is an egotist. He relinquishes all the personal values which only marriage and family can establish, and receives no substitute for them. And this is true even of the prosperous bachelor who tries to forget the gap in his life by leading a gay life with boon companions and in the end dies unmourned, leaving only greedy heirs to quarrel over his estate. It is equally true of the priest who, indifferent to the real purpose of his celibacy—a loving surrender to the importunity of his parishioners—locks himself up moodily in his presbytery. "One is not permitted to give up the state of wedlock just because it seems distasteful, even though there may be some who consider this attitude moral, instead of calling it by its right name, downright cowardice fit to be accursed. And one should not fly from the 'world' because it is cruel and unsatisfying, in order to take up a monastic life, for if one did this, where would 'sacrifice' come in? A man only makes a sacrifice when he gives up that which he really values. Only when the world is fully recognized with all its lure and beauty is it a worthy exchange, a thing to be gladly renounced for an eternal world of still greater beauty and wonder" (R. Allers).

The extension of family love to the whole of God's kingdom is typified in the liturgy by the bishop's ring, which signifies marriage embracing the whole family of God. This thought is still more beautifully brought out by the *Pontificale Romanum* where, in the preface to the Virginal Blessing,[14] the following passage occurs: "Without in any way reflecting on the honorable state of matrimony and the blessing that rests upon it, there are nevertheless pious souls who, renouncing the physical union which men and women enter into, strive to possess themselves of the mystery which that union embraces. They do not imitate what happens in marriage but offer up their whole love to the mystery which marriage represents." We may see by this that marriage and celibacy are by no means antagonistic to each other. Virginity only makes sense and derives value insofar as it matches marriage or even excels it in representing the union of Christ with His heavenly realm.

Such virginal love cannot possibly disdain its "sensual" sister; on the contrary, it ennobles and sanctifies the latter. From Plato down to the present day, countless thinkers both inside and outside Christendom have looked upon this highest love as a purely "Platonic" concept: that is to say, one which is quite spiritual, without the slightest trace of sensual meaning. Yet that is a pure abstraction. The only kind of love a human being is capable of is human love, and its nature must therefore necessarily be sensual-spiritual—it cannot escape being in some way bound up with the senses. When a Sister of Mercy loves the child which is entrusted to her care, the value of that love is not diminished because it takes effect with physical contact, with spoken words of coaxing affection; on the contrary, it becomes more natural and precious. Of course, it must be taken for granted that the relationship radiates true, inward, supernatural love, and that it is not lavished simply on one favorite but extends equally to all children with whom the subject comes into contact. Even love of God is not completely abstract and spiritual. That is why the Love of God dwelt among us in the shape of man, "ut, dum visibiliter Deum cognoscimus, per hunc in invisibilium amorem rapiamur"—"so that we, recognizing God visibly, may be drawn to love the invisible" (Christmas Preface).

NOTES

1. *Scholastik, loc. cit.*
2. *Zeitschrift für katholische Theologie, loc. cit.*
3. *Ibid.*, p. 441.
4. "Si quis invocatione humana gratiam Dei dicit posse conferri, non autem ipsam gratiam facere, ut invocetur a nobis, contradicit Isaiæ Prophetæ, vel Apostolo idem dicenti: *'Inventus sum a non quærentibus me; palam apparui his, qui me non interrogabant.'* "—DB 176; "Si quis, ut a peccato purgemur, voluntatem nostram Deum expectare contendit, non autem, ut etiam, purgari velimus, per Sancti Spiritus infusionem et operationem in nos fieri confitetur, resistit ipsi Spiritui Sancto per Salomonem dicenti: *'Præparatur voluntas a Domino,'* et Apostolo salubriter praedicanti: *'Deus est, qui operatur in vobis et velle et perficere pro bona voluntate.'* "—DB 177.
5. "*Quales nos diligat Deus.* Tales nos amat Deus, quales futuri sumus ipsius dono, non quales sumus nostro merito."—DB 185.
6. *Zeitschrift für katholische Theologie, loc. cit.*
7. *Nature of Sanctity* (London, 1933).
8. See Hornstein-Faller, *loc. cit.*, p. 50.
9. *Nichomachean Ethics,* 1153^b, 1-1154^a, 7.
10. J.Mausbach, *Ehe- und Kindersegen,* p. 113.
11. The expression, *membra inhonesta,* "uncomely parts," certainly does occur in I Corinthians 12:23, but in quite a different sense and connection than that in which it is used by many moralists. St. Paul is here not referring to chastity at all, but to the organic connection of the parts of the human body, among which the less important have to serve the more important, but must not on that account be underrated. St. Paul uses this as an illustration of the unity of the Church despite the variety of its members.
12. F. Walter, *loc. cit.*, p. 13.
13. See the penetrating essay, "Sexus, Eros, Liebe," of O. Karrer, S.J., Hornstein-Faller, *op. cit.*, p. 159.
14. A. Wintersig, "Die Jungfrauenweihe," *Religiöse Quellenschriften,* 6 (Düsseldorf, 1926).

CHAPTER 6

The Teaching of *Parvitas Materiae* and the Singling out of the Sixth Commandment

ALL moral theologians unanimously agree that the greater or lesser gravity of a sin depends upon two factors. Objectively, its importance is determined by that of the commandment or virtue against which it transgresses. Since love takes precedence over all other virtues, sins against the commandment of love must be the most grievous of all.[1] Thomas Aquinas again sets up a scale by which offenses can be assessed within the framework of love. He bases his deductions on the question whether the sins concerned offend directly against God, or against His members, or against His Commandments.[2] The greatest of all sins is hatred of God, and the worst offenses against brotherly love are the consequences of this sin. From a purely objective point of view, therefore, the slanderer is more immoral than one who transgresses the so-called "moral code." A gossip, a tittle-tattle, one who spreads false rumors or makes mischief to disturb the peace of a community, is more immoral than a wanton or a libertine. Sins of licentiousness only become grievous when they offend against love, as, for instance, in the breaking of matrimonial vows or in seduction. Thomas repeatedly emphasizes that sins against the first table are more serious than sins against the second,[3] and that sins of the flesh are less grave than sins of the spirit, even if, by man's own standard, the former are more shameful than the latter.[4]

Subjectively considered, the gravity of a sin is determined according to the amount of free will that goes to the commission of it. "The more determined the will, the more calculated the bad intentions, the greater the sin." The gravity of the sin is always affected by contributory causes which must be taken into consideration, as, for instance, ignorance or anything that may have interfered with freedom of will in making the final decision. If the act under consideration is completely involuntary, it loses its sinful character altogether.[5] With uncommonly penetrating psychology, the great theologian, in the *Summa Theologica* (1-2, q. 73, a. 5), poses the question—Whether carnal sins are of less guilt than spiritual sins, like hatred or pride. He gives three reasons: 1. From the sinner's standpoint (*ex parte subjecti*), mortal sin is in essence a turning away from God in order to give oneself up to a created thing. But this movement reaches its fulfillment in the spirit of man; therefore, sins of the spirit are a radical departure from the eternal goal because, in the first place, they are a severance from God and, in the second place, a cleaving to the created thing. Sins of the flesh, on the other hand, are primarily an impulse toward some created thing and only in a secondary sense a turning from God. They aim at the satisfaction of the body, and the breaking of the commandment is merely a consequence of this.

2. From the standpoint of the object against which the sin is committed (*ex parte ejus in quem peccatur*),

sins of the spirit directly affect God or the sinner's neighbor; those of the flesh are only an offense against his own person. According to the order of love (*ordo caritatis*), God and one's neighbor must be loved more than one's own body.

3. From the standpoint of motive (*ex parte motivi*). The more violent the inner urge, the more excusable the fault (*quanto est gravius impulsivum ad peccandum, tanto homo minus peccat*). Now, the sex impulse is greatly augmented because of the desire that is inherent in the human make-up. By establishing this, St. Thomas takes the exactly opposite line to those authors who blame the "elementary violence" of the sexual instinct for the extreme gravity of licentious sin. Of course, no one would deny that chastity is a serious matter; but the impetus of the sexual instinct tends to cloud the reason and to weaken will power more than in the case of offenses committed in cold blood, so that, even when the case is a serious one, there cannot commonly be a question of an absolutely complete consent of the will.

Modern practice—much to its detriment—has departed in many ways from the skillful treatment which this classical author of scholastic theology brought to bear upon sins against the Sixth Commandment. The tendency to place sexual behavior in the foreground of moral values, which set in after the Great Schism, influenced pastoral practice profoundly; nor did it pass the science of moral theology by without leaving some trace of its coloring. Here, too, it led to a greater strictness in the attitude toward sins of unchastity. Strangely enough two crosscurrents, which on other questions were in hearty opposition, met here on common ground.

Moral theologians of the Age of Enlightenment, not even excluding men like Stattler, Ruf, and so on, who tried hard to withstand the prevailing tide of opinion and to safeguard the supernatural viewpoint, are exceedingly strict in their weighing up of sexual sins; even the otherwise gentle Sailer is quite unlike his usual self in this respect.[6] The opposite current of thought is represented by St. Alphonsus Liguori and his school, which took up arms valiantly against the "morality of reason" but also viewed questions affecting the Sixth Commandment with ruthless vigor. The reproaches leveled at this saintly theologian are well known. They are not all justified, and the constant repetition of these attacks need by no means be taken as a proof of their validity. It was precisely this holy man who castigated the exaggerations of contemporary and earlier moral theologians and brought a much milder attitude to bear on marriage, just as he was active in opposing many other extreme views. The faults for which he is so often blamed could, indeed, be placed at the door of many of his commentators, for he has been much misinterpreted.[7]

Even before the influence of Alphonsus began to be felt, there had been a tightening up of the general attitude toward sins against the Sixth Commandment. This found expression in teachings which the saint is incorrectly supposed to have originated. It is quite true that these teachings are reflected in the moral theology of Alphonsus but not in the sense of isolating the Sixth Commandment as a thing apart, a later development which was far from the saint's intention. The teaching is called *parvitas materiæ*. It teaches that every conscious trespass against the Sixth Commandment is of vital importance and therefore must be regarded as a grevious sin insofar as it is committed with full knowledge and will. This puts the Sixth Commandment in a class of its own; for when the other commandments are broken, the resulting sin can, under certain circumstances, be venial. If it is a minor matter like the purloining of a few cents, or the telling of a little fib, and so on, the sin may be considered venial. But there is no question of an objective factor of this kind in the case of the Sixth Commandment. Here there can be nothing of secondary importance. Even the slightest unchaste thought, if entertained consciously and willingly, is a mortal sin.

All moral theologians agree with St. Alphonsus that all acts outside of marriage, which have the satisfaction of sensual lust (*delectatio venerea*) as their aim, must be regarded as serious sins. The teaching of *parvitas materiae* is in this respect unquestionably right and agrees with a decision given by Alexander VII (DB 1140). For our Lord Himself says: "Whosover shall look on a woman to lust after her, hath already committed adultery with her in his heart" (Matt. 5: 28).

Nevertheless, there is a great difference of opinion among moral theologians in arriving at a verdict on acts in which the satisfaction proceeds from natural inclination of the senses without deliberately evil intent. Clearly, the interplay of spiritual and sensual emotions in the human make-up may produce conditions which sweep a man off his feet under pressure of passion or strain, so that the danger of sexual satisfaction can sometimes occur without any cooperation on his part. Alphonsus here follows the sterner course and stretches the basic idea of *parvitas materiae* to cover such acts, though they belong to the sensual sphere. He holds that the sin is in itself grievous "because, owing to the nature of man through original sin, it is morally impossible for him to enjoy a purely natural pleasurable sensation involving emotional excitement without carnal lust when such people have the inclination and capacity or when such acts occur under pressure of passion or strain" (*Theologia Moralis*, lib. IV, tract. IV, no. 416).[8]

With all due respect for the authority of Alphonsus, this application of the basic idea is rejected by moral theologians of today. The well-known Münster authority, J. Mausbach (in *Katholische Moraltheologie,* III, 98), writes: "It is important not to include every kind of pleasurable sensation, not even if it happens to be sexual, in the category of evil lust (*delectatio venerea*). Quite apart from pleasures of the senses such as delight in colors, music and so on . . . there are inner desires and emotional capacities, permitted impressions and yearnings which may occupy themselves with sensual, and even to some extent with sexual matters, as, for instance, the universal attraction of the sexes to one another, and that reaching-out for love which, despite its sensual aspect, remains a permissible and noble passion. This applies no less to the erotic, piquant, fanciful sensations which overstep the thin borderline of propriety but are still essentially different from *delectatio venerea* and only venial (*delectatio spiritualis-sensibilis*)." And the Tübingen theologian, O. Schilling, whose work is concerned with St. Thomas Aquinas, distinguishes from deliberate lust (*Lehrbuch der Moraltheologie,* I, 312), that is to say, from "*complacentia,*" that "sense of pleasure (*placentia*) which springs from some physiological or psychological cause and can, of course, develop into lust in the fullest sense of the word. For instance, an emotional experience that proceeds from an object capable of rousing *delectatio venerea,* such as intellectual friendship between the sexes. Here reference is not to the purely emotional sensation, which does not enter into the argument, but to sensuality, which can very easily develop into sensual excitement. The acts concerned, when unpremeditated, are venial sins provided the more serious temptations to which they may lead are resisted." Similarly, on p. 313, he writes: "These acts [i.e., deliberate sensual satisfaction] while they are mortal sins because of full knowledge, can be excused on the grounds of *parvitas materiae* because these acts are a consequence of a not-in-itself-sinful lust that was actually willed. The acts concerned could include embracing, kissing, meaning glances, loose conversation and similar means of exciting sexual passion."

The Würzburg moralist, F. A. Göpfert (*Moraltheologie*, 9th Edition, revised by K. Staab, II, 304), confines the clause concerning *parvitas materiae* to sexual lust "consciously sought, or deliberately permitted, with complete free will," while indirectly desired lust can in certain circumstances rank as venial, according to the degree of consent. This view is represented by Jerome Noldin, S.J., who quite rightly calls attention to the fact that, in the case of indirectly desired *delectatio venerea,* the will consents to the cause which called the lust into being and not to the lust itself. This influence of cause on the emergence of lust may, however, be a remote one, in which case the sin remains a grievous one. The newest *Lehrbuch* of the Tübingen moral theologist, Stelzenberg (1953), excludes the *parvitas materiae* from the Sixth Commandment without further objection (p. 237).

We are thus faced with a situation in which distinguished authorities on moral theology at the present time place severe restriction on the application of the *parvitas materiae* clause in matters of sex, or ignore it altogether. But this attitude robs the clause of the very virtue which is given to it in the catechism and repeatedly underlined from the pulpit, and boils down its meaning to this: every deliberate sexual indulgence outside of marriage is a grievous sin. But this interpretation of the phrase would with parallel logic apply to any of the commandments. The matter is of major importance when the transgression "affects the formal object, i.e., virtue" (Mausbach, I, 237); or, as Schilling still more clearly expresses it: "when a fundamental principle of a religious, social or individual nature has been deliberately violated" (I, 247). We should not look upon the Sixth Commandment as being unique with regard to *parvitas materiae;* any sin that offends an indivisible object, that is, one that does not lend itself to qualification —for instance, apostasy, blasphemy, treachery, murder, and so on—is incapable of being modified on the grounds of *parvitas materiae.*

The indifference shown toward the contraction of the *parvitas materiae* clause should give rise to very serious reflection. Most modern preachers are content to accept its narrowest sense in their explanations. Without any attempt to distinguish between them, the words "moral," "sexual," and "unchaste" are used indiscriminately, treated as synonymous, and freely exchanged for one another. In order to stress the dangers of unchastity, every variety of sensual lust is degraded into a capital sin. Göpfert very rightly utters a warning against this sort of exaggeration: "This proves the great error many preachers, teachers and priests in the confessional fall into, when they indiscriminately pronounce all sins against the Sixth Commandment to be mortal sins . . . if all sins against chastity are grievous, that does not apply to sins against shame and decency, which can lead to unchastity. But since ordinary, uneducated people cannot distinguish between unchastity, sensuality and indecency, it is not good to stress that all sins of *luxuria directa* are mortal. Such clumsiness may lead to many mortal sins being committed through confusion of conscience or to some supposedly grave trespass committed half involuntarily, being sacrilegiously withheld in confession. At the very least much fear and many scruples will be awakened" (*Moraltheologie* II, 307).

But the most serious consequence of all must emerge when the *parvitas materiae* clause leads to a formal isolation of the Sixth Commandment. By setting it apart, the idea takes root that this commandment is framed on different and more serious laws than all the others. In his *Standespredigten,* P. Weninger writes (p. 29): "The sin [unchastity] is a crime, and everything appertaining to it is grievous . . . a man can be somewhat proud, somewhat overbearing or envious . . . and be guilty of no mortal sin. But he dare not be unchaste. If he is, everything done in that connection will be a mortal sin." This sort of thing makes one think.

Even where there is no direct inclination to treat every sexual offense as a mortal sin on the basis of the *parvitas materiae* clause, it should not be forgotten that in the Sixth Commandment the subjective factor, namely, full perception and freedom of will power, is in general not so much in evidence as it is in the case of all the other commandments. The passion inherent in the urge lessens perception and hinders will power. As we have seen above, St. Thomas gives these very reasons for pronouncing unchastity a minor transgression. "The more insistent the urge, the less grievous the fault" (*quanto est gravius impulsivum ad peccandum, tanto homo minus peccat*—1-2, q. 73, a. 5). St. Alphonsus himself agrees with this in his general morality (Lib. II, *Tractatus de actibus humanis,* art. III, p. 325) where he writes that the preliminary impulse "diminishes the free will of the transaction, because the impulse has completely clouded the perception and distorted it. Indeed there are times when free will ceases to function because the perception is completely obscured by the overpowering impulse." St. Alphonsus certainly knows all about the *parvitas materiae* clause, but does not by any means confine it to the Sixth Commandment in the sense of isolating that particular one. He makes no concessions to a sin which is incapable of being minimized "ubi ob parvitatem non excusatur ratio offensionis" (Lib. II, *Tractatus de Peccatis*, cap. II, 56), and puts unchastity on a par with lack of faith, hatred of God, simony, treachery, and blasphemy. Moralists do not give this teaching the grave emphasis preachers are fond of adding to it. Mausbach, for instance, does not mention it at all; Schilling refers to it only incidentally. Here, too, practice ought to draw a little closer to theory. The phrase *parvitas materiae* is very subject to misinterpretation and, if not exactly explained from the pulpit and in school, it must seem either incomprehensible or inapplicable to most cases. Inadequately explained, and laden with limitations, it is calculated to do more harm than good.

St. Thomas Aquinas knew nothing whatever about this problem of *parvitas materiae*, a fact which, in view of the all-embracing thoroughness of this greatest of all theologians, deserves our particular attention. The reason must be sought in the viewpoint from which he approached his teachings—a viewpoint totally different from that of the casuistic moral theology of later times. Basing his method on Aristotle, St. Thomas dealt with the commandments as they came within the framework of the four cardinal virtues: wisdom, justice, valor, and temperance. He makes these four fundamental virtues the basis on which the whole scaffolding of natural morality is built up. Amplified in Christian life by the supernatural virtues of faith, hope, and charity, they form a combination of seven which should determine the fundamental behavior of every baptized person. All other moral virtues are only relative, and represent different outward expressions of the application of this conduct to the realities of life.[9] Chastity is one of the outward expressions (*partes subjectivae*) of the fourth cardinal virtue, temperance. It maintains good order in the sphere of the sensual appetites by controlling the sexual instinct and confining it to its divinely ordained purpose.

A man can transgress against the virtue of *temperantia,* as regards moderation and control of his impulses, in two different ways: by complete surrender to his appetites or by occasional lapses (*Sum. Th.,* 2-2, q. 156). The first class of sin—*intemperantia*—is complete, fundamental contempt of all law and order in the realm of sensual impulse. The second class of offense—*incontinentia*—is a temporary lapse in control, a passing surrender to overpowering passion. There is little difference in the outward form both sins take, but a great deal of difference in their inner attitude to the reasonable control of sex life. Complete surrender to carnal desires and abandonment of all self-control are the marks of *intemperantia;* here the will to keep a check on sexual impulses has been completely undermined. *Incontinentia,* on the other hand, denoted that the fundamental principles have not been abandoned. Only the will power, because of the reason being temporarily blinded by passion, has been weakened, thus enabling temptation to triumph. "In the libertine (*intemperatus*) the inclination to sin has become a habit (*habitus*). The incontinent person (*incontinens*), on the other hand, is only prone to sudden passion. The passion passes, but as the fundamental conduct remains more or less fixed, the offender quickly repents when the passion is spent. In the case of a libertine this does not happen; on the contrary, he glories in the sin, because it has become second nature to him" (art. 3). Lack of control is like a sudden fever that "rises out of the excitement of the blood" and is, therefore, conditioned by physiological causes. Licentiousness, on the other hand, is more like consumption, being a chronic disease (ad 1). The conversion of the libertine is, therefore, much more difficult than of one who is merely incontinent (ad 2). At the same time, the measure of lust is not uncommonly greater in the case of the incontinent than of the licentious; but since the latter fall into sin at the slightest temptation, their offense is greater than that of the former (ad 3). We may see by these examples that St. Thomas went into the greatest possible detail, passing even individual sins in review. In coming to a conclusion on the greater or lesser degree of sinfulness, he is solely influenced by the attitude the sinner brings to bear on his offense. The passionate but essentially honest lover, momentarily carried away, is never pronounced guilty to the same degree as the blasé worldling who has to whip up his libido artificially and has long ago thrown all principles and propriety to the winds. But of course there is always the danger that often-repeated *incontinentia* may eventually end up as *intemperantia*, so that it is very hard to determine where one begins and the other finishes.

Nowhere is the difference between the classical, psychological, and securely anchored morality of Thomas Aquinas and the mechanical casuistry of later times more clearly revealed than in the treatment of the Sixth Commandment. St. Thomas judges the moral quality of a proceeding, not by the details of the act, but by the attitude of the person who executes it. But the theory of *parvitas materiae* is concerned first and foremost with the act itself. Naturally, the moralist in this case also has to take into account the conditions from which the act emerged. But these are mere appendages which give the act this, that, or the other color according to whether they sharpened or blunted perception, thereby firing or impeding the will. The decisive factor is the act itself and its greater or lesser fulfillment. On this basis, later morality carefully distinguishes between the *actus completus* and the *actus incompletus* (*see* Alphonsus Liguori, *op. cit.*, lib. IV, tract 4, cap. 2, no. 412). Although the results may in many instances be identical, the standpoint of Thomas is still diametrically opposed to that of the later casuists. Thomas starts off with the living personality and judges in accordance with what he finds there. The casuists take the act as their starting point and judge the person committing it by that. Thomas makes "being" his basis; his successors place the accent on "doing." St. Thomas takes the view that the identical act can be of greater or lesser gravity, the distinction depending upon the extent to which the fundamental principles of conduct are repudiated or merely temporarily in abeyance. There can be no doubt that the method of Aquinas is far more penetrating and takes the individual characteristics of personality far more comprehensively into account, while followers of the later school are preoccupied with specializing to such an extent that the human being hardly counts.

The differentiation Thomas makes is far more than a mere scholastic distinction. For the moral judgment of sins against chastity, it is of practical and decisive importance. There is surely an immense difference between the sin of a young man who, genuinely attracted, forgets himself in a moment of passion but is fully prepared to stand by the consequences—and a confirmed debauchee who looks upon every female as fair game and seeks his own satisfaction without any deep affection and with no sense of responsibility whatsoever. Later morality, with its theory of *parvitas materiae*, regards both offenses as completely equal, under the title of *actus completus,* so that many priests are tempted, in the confessional, to lump them together although, both psychologically and morally, they are utterly distinct. Individualism, with its "tendency to subdivide, and its complete lack of an over-all view" (A. M. Weiss), contrived in later years to spread its influence even to moral theology, so that many theologians who believed themselves to be combating it were actually caught by its insidious ideas. The problem of *parvitas materiae,* which is at the root of the probabalist controversy, also paved the way for an acceptance of this passion for reducing everything to isolated acts. St. Thomas would be quite out of his depth here because he knew nothing about this science of "splitting up"—it was quite out of his line. Nowadays, Catholic morality could profit, just as much as dogma has profited, by referring back to the great man Aquinas and his classical theology.

The preachers of the Middle Ages castigated offenses against chastity severely; of that we have ample proof. But nowhere do we find them making exceptions in their judgment of these sins, any more than the catechisms and confessional handbooks of that time treat offenses against the Sixth Commandment any more rigorously, or any less severely, than the breach of any other commandment. It is true that Berthold of Ratisbon (d. 1272) often describes unchastity as "the greatest of all sins," [10] but he is inconsistent enough to mention greed in the very same sermons as being even worse than unchastity—"This is the very worst, and most evil, and destructive." Then again he speaks of murder as "the worst of all sins." His thirty-fourth sermon, "Concerning our Lord on the Cross," deals with the order of virtues, giving the theological ones priority over those which are merely moral, and here he appears to consider faith more important than love: "the highest of all virtues is faith, beautiful, righteous Christian faith." Then he goes on to describe joyful love as the next in order of importance. In fact, it is obvious that Brother Berthold is out to captivate his hearers by his rhetoric rather than to present them with systematic theology. He faces sexual facts in the unself-conscious manner of his time, and few preachers are more emphatic in their high esteem of marriage. "God has fortified marriage with *more blessings than any Order* the world ever was blessed with—more than that of the bare-footed monks, more than that of the preaching friars or the grey monks; none of these can compare with the sacred bond of matrimony. As this Order cannot be dispensed with, God has commanded it; all the other Orders He merely recommends" (J. Muller, *loc. cit.*, 384).

Geiler von Kaysersberg, who died in 1510 at Strasbourg, uses hard words and is a very severe critic; but, on the whole, the mean and the haughty fare worse at his hands than do the unchaste. The same may be said of the famous Viennese court preacher, Abraham a Sancta Clara, who has a liking for blunt speech and, in exquisite little verbal vignettes, paints the failings of his listeners as he tongue-lashes them. His kindhearted and understanding humor is seen at its best in the way he handles sexual failings. When we compare these three important preachers with those of later times, we are struck by the way they handle offenses against chastity, treating them seriously, to be sure, but without that special emphasis which would give them an aura of extraordinary importance. It never occurs to any of them to treat these sins as if they were in a class apart, declaring their evil to be out of all proportion to the wickedness of all other sins. The opposite tendency sets in with Hunolt who died in 1709 and, therefore, is a later contemporary of Sancta Clara's. What a difference between the works of these two distinguished preachers! The Viennese speaker sparkles with originality; he has at his command a bubbling abundance of apt comparisons, intermingled with baroque crudity; every now and then lightning breaks in, the fun ceases, and the thunder of condemnation breaks forth; but it is all informed with great good humor, never leaving the poor, chastized sinner without one final word of comfort. The cathedral preacher of Trier is little behind his Viennese colleague in the richness and variety of his imagery; he, too, has a wealth of imagination and a deep fund of wisdom to draw upon. The measured rhetoric of this speaker has proved a more lasting pattern for his successors than the baroque ornamentation of Sancta Clara; but he always speaks in sober earnest and his utterances are mercilessly severe. He grinds the sinner into the very ashes with his censorious tongue and offers little in the way of encouragement. His immeasurable severity, which has in it little kindness and never a glint of humor, is most clearly brought out by his sermons on the Sixth Commandment—these would do credit to any Puritan! He calls unchastity the greatest and most grievous of all sins—"the one which, more than any other, besmirches the soul"—it "behaves in a bestial fashion, so that nothing God-like is to be found in it" (p. 221). "There is no sin that offends God more than the crime of unchastity and impure love" (p. 255). He describes it as being practically incapable of conversion (p. 234): "I know well that with God nothing is impossible; but if anything were impossible for Him, it would be the conversion of a sinner who has given himself over to lust and is completely enslaved by impure love" (p. 244). For this reason he did not even wish to preach to the unchaste, on whom he considered all warnings were wasted. He only wished to preach to others so that they might guard against this sin (p. 252). He even goes so far as to say that he looks upon unchastity as "a greater crime than the denial of faith and the apostasy of a Christian" (p. 257). To substantiate this amazing statement, which contradicts all moral theology, he not only erroneously quotes St. Thomas Aquinas (p. 256), but also the African writer, Tertullian, whose opinions he repeats verbally and calmly appropriates (p. 257). Herein he overlooks the fact that these passages belong to the work called *De pudicitia* (cap. 22), in which the zealous Montanist bitterly attacks the Edict on Penance issued by Pope Callistus [11]—the very work in which Tertullian tries to justify his resignation from the Church because of his disagreement with the pope in an attitude toward penance which he considered too lenient, especially as it affected sins against chastity. Here we stand face to face with the regrettable fact that opinions which were rejected by the early Church as being in open opposition to the Church's teaching on account of their heretical rigor can reappear in the present day in a widely-used work which is accepted as an expression of the Catholic stand on matters of morality. Surely there can be no greater proof of the present author's contention that a very unhealthy narrowing down of the moral concept set in between the seventeenth and eighteenth centuries and is still receiving support from many a Catholic pulpit. It is no mere coincidence that the oldest German representative of this tendency had to resort to the Montanist, Tertullian, who, even in those early days, preened himself on the rigor of his "superior morality" (*De pud.* cap. 1). The cathedral preacher of Trier had an enormous following in his own time, and his volume of sermons which, on account of their masterly use of the language and their otherwise excellent contents must be regarded as classics, continue to exert an enormous influence. Until recent years, they were still being constantly reprinted.

Hunolt is not, however, the originator of these exaggerations. The cathedral preacher of Trier owed much to the inspiration of French classics in pulpit oratory, notably the works of L. Bourdaloue (d. 1704) and J. B. Massillon (d. 1742).[12] Bourdaloue's sermon on the third Sunday of Lent ("Sur l'impurité"), in particular, served as Hunolt's model for his approach to the Sixth Commandment. The erroneous quotation of the passage from St. Thomas, as well as the misquotation of St. Bernard, may be traced to Bourdaloue, and the same is true of the idea that sins against chastity are incapable of repentance; Bourdaloue calls them "plus irremissible." The detailed use of Tertullian's work, *De pudicitia,* can also be traced back to the same source. Bourdaloue finds the reasons whereby the African writer seeks to justify his contention that sins against chastity are unforgivable (and thereby also to justify his resignation from the Church) "very sound" (*très solides*), even though Tertullian drew exaggerated conclusions from them. Bourdaloue maintains that sins against chastity are, not fundamentally, but practically almost unforgivable "since the sinner creates a condition of unreadiness for penitence." While with all his sympathy for Tertullian's Montanist teaching (the African apostate, when he left the Catholic Church, went over to the sect founded by Montanus), he does at least mention that author's falling away from the Church; but his German imitator omits this trifling detail and treats the heretic as if he were a fully accredited teacher of the Church! The connection between Catholic rigorism (which through Hunolt gained access for the first time to German pulpits) and French Jansenism is clearly demonstrated by these examples. Bourdaloue was more expansive on this question than Massillon, from whom Hunolt also borrowed (compare the first part of Massillon's speech, "On the very small number of the chosen"). It is somewhat piquant to reflect that at the French court, where both Bourdaloue and Massillon were employed as court preachers, not only the most shameless licentiousness, but also the most exaggerated prudery on sexual matters existed side by side—*les extrêmes se touchent.*

It might of course appear, on reflection, that all these pulpit fulminations about chastity and offenses against chastity are more an expression of rhetorical fashion than of deep-seated moral convictions. One should not "take these exaggerations quite so seriously. It is an old-established custom among preachers always to treat the virtue which happens to be uppermost at the moment as the most important of all the virtues. And the same applies to sin; the one which engages most current attention is always the worst, and there is really no serious intention of shattering the whole hierarchy of values." [13] Yes, it may be that for pedagogic reasons such exaggeration is to some extent tolerated. Just as, in archery, the arrow must be aimed a little higher than the target to allow for the natural law of gravity, similarly it is advisable to emphasize moral duties a little more sharply than necessary so that they may reach their target, even if only with a minimum of effect.

But there is great danger in this method of attempting to let one extreme cancel another out. It may be necessary, in certain circumstances, to drive home a particular lesson with special force in order to suit individual mentalities. St. Francis de Sales excuses the hermit Hilarion, in his contention that cleanliness was a superfluous refinement in a penitential garment, by explaining that when the anchorite used these words, they were addressed to degenerate courtiers who needed jolting to attention. "Those who wish to correct a sapling that has grown crooked adopt similar methods—they do not content themselves with propping it upright, but bend it a little in the opposite direction, so that it may find the exact central line for itself." [14] But the usefulness of such tactical exaggeration is doubtful, even in mundane matters, for in the long run everything overemphasized will tend to swing over to the other extreme. In the religious and moral sphere they are especially dangerous, since they can easily lead to rigorism and heresy. And we are not here concerned with an ordinary educational process in which first one virtue and then another—now justice, now chastity, now industry, or any other duty momentarily in the foreground—is stressed. Here we are faced with the fact that ever and again it is chastity that is singled out for veneration as the highest virtue, while any and every offense against chastity is treated as the most grievous and unforgivable sin. This is no longer a question of pedagogic method; it is a false principle! Berthold of Ratisbon did not always describe unchastity as the greatest sin, as we can see from the example we have already quoted; and apart from that, it is just possible that his superlatives crept in through the pen of his transcriber, for he did not write his sermons personally. Exaggerations are far less excusable in a sermon than they are in a speech before an ordinary public assembly, or in a political address. It is the preacher's duty to publish the Word of God, without any addition. Every amplification that springs from human thought is bound to weaken its effect. Anyone who believes that moral duties can be driven home more effectively by special emphasis, runs the risk of building up a warped conscience. His method befogs the border line between venial and mortal sin and, in the end, his constant superlatives will blunt the very warnings he is trying to emphasize. To fall back on "old-established customs" is a very lame excuse and contradicts the historical facts. What we really need is to go back to the exactitude of our forefathers and to that scrupulous phraseology in matters of faith and moral teaching which sometimes—quite incorrectly—appears merely pedantic to the modern mind.

NOTES

1. St. Thomas Aquinas, *Summa Theologica,* 1–2, q. 73, a. 3-5.
2. *Ibid.,* 2–2, q. 20, a. 3.
3. *Ibid.,* 1–2, q. 110, a. 6.
4. *Ibid.,* 1–2, q. 73, a. 5; 2–2, q. 116, a. 2, ad 2; q. 142, a. 4, ad 2; q. 144, a. 2; etc.
5. *Ibid.,* 1–2, q. 73, a. 6.
6. J. M. Sailer, *Handbuch der Christlichen Moral,* II, 194.
7. D. Lindner, *loc. cit.,* p. 177.
8. "Dubium secundum est, an detur parvitas materiæ in delectatione sensibile sive naturali, nempe si quis delectetur de contracta manus femininae, prout de contactu rei lenis, puta rosa, panni serici et similis? . . . Secunda tamen sententia negat . . . et hanc puto omnino tenendam . . . quia ob corruptam naturam est moraliter impossibile habere illam naturalem delectationem, quin delectatio carnalis et venerea sentiatur, maxime a personis ad copulam aptis, et maxime si actus isti habeantur cum aliquo affectu et mora."
9. J. Pieper, *Ueber das Christliche Menschenbild* (Munich, n.d.).
10. Göbel, *Die Missionspredigten des Franziskaners Berthold von Regensberg in jetziger Schriftsprache* (Ratisbon, 1873). See especially sermon 7, on the angels; no. 14, on the seven very grievous sins; and also sermon 6.
11. It may also be that, not Callistus, but Bishop Agrippinus of Carthage is called the "bishop of bishops" by Tertullian.
12. The author is indebted to the friendly assistance of Dr. F. Zillmann of Heydebreck for these references showing Hunolt's dependence on the French preachers.
13. *Zeitschrift für katholische Theologie, loc. cit.*
14. F. Walter, *loc. cit.,* p. 81.

CHAPTER 7

Pastoral Deductions

THE pastoral function is to discover ways and means by which the truths of revelation can be applied to the Christian's daily life and conduct. A pastor must keep himself on the right track by constantly referring to the eternal truths which hold good for all time—this is as important as the maritime rule which makes a mariner direct his course by the stars. No matter what storms he may encounter, the seaman can trust the stars, which never change in their courses. It is the same with the eternal truths of revelation.

If love is the greatest of all commandments, this truth must stand in the forefront of Christian moral teaching—in pulpit, in catechism, in asceticism, in the confessional. In short, the one task of the kingdom of God here on earth is to express this truth.

This book does not set out in any way to minimize the importance of sins against chastity or to advocate any kind of laxity in the treatment of burning questions which the sex problem—rightly or wrongly—has called into being. But it *is* concerned with examining this question in relation to the rest of morality, so that it may be restored to its proper place in the framework as a whole. If it is true that love is the pivot on which all the laws of morality turn, pastoral duty plainly demands that the sexual problem be centered in the very heart of the *caritas* concept. This must be the object of all teaching, in school, from the pulpit, and through the sacrament of penance; moreover, it must be actually incorporated in the personal life of the priest. Since sins against love are the most grievous of all, it is essential that they should be branded as such in pastoral activity as a whole. This is not a matter of bringing such leniency to bear on sins against chastity as to give the impression that they are practically harmless. The priest must wage war on them as earnestly as before. But he will be gravely at fault if he fails to bring the same severity to bear on other sins which are even more grave than this one.

It is one of the most essential truths of the Christian faith that a sin consists not so much in the purely objective commission or omission of an act, as in the fact that the act springs fundamentally from a definite direction of the human will. Our Lord constantly calls attention to this inner motivation, in contrast with its outer fulfillment. Take, for instance, the purely ritualistic "sin" or "cleanliness" to which Mosaic law attached so much importance, and which was the ground for so much pharisaical boasting. "Woe to you, Scribes and Pharisees, hypocrites; because you make clean the outside of the cup and of the dish, but within you are full of rapine and uncleanness" (Matt. 23:25). The danger of the concept of sin degenerating into a mere outward form is nowhere more noticeable than in the evaluation of the Sixth Commandment because, precisely here, the human and the divine standards are brought into most glaring opposition. Superficial thinking, even among Christians, will always tend to confuse scandal with sin. From a purely human standpoint, it will always appear to simple, uneducated people that failings which stir up most public excitement should also be most severely condemned. Of course, the preacher who readily falls in with this general opinion and freely endorses it will always be certain of popularity. He will be able to count on the solid support of the more respectable members of his congregation when he lets fly against "immoral" modes, "immoral" associations, "immoral" dances and pleasure resorts. But a great many of them will listen far less complacently if he brings his ammunition to bear on backbiting, gossip, scandal, and other forms of polite recreation which demonstrate anything but brotherly love. Yet, all things being equal, both the Scriptures and tradition agree that the latter offenses are far more vile and sinful than the former. It is the way of the world to be more shocked at *turpe* than at *malitia*—to boggle at the shameful, and let the sinful go. The same spirit in the human make-up leads people to judge by outward appearances—to measure piety and morality by quantitative yardsticks. Piety by this standard becomes a matter of the greatest number of prayers and outward observances; morals are judged by the esteem a person can earn by conforming to convention. This worldly spirit will always persist as long as there are sinful, superficial people; and no religion, however noble, is free from it, not even the most exalted of them all, Christianity, which should fill mankind with the spirit of inwardness. It is this worldly spirit that will always be ready to cast stones at the adulteress and to pronounce the Pharisee a very fine fellow—moreover, it will be conscious of having public opinion firmly on its side. Nevertheless, it is the preacher's duty to follow in the footsteps of his Divine Master by challenging public opinion, instead of lending it his support.

If, in the face of this worldly spirit, one adopts a

somewhat broad-minded attitude toward sexual offenses while condemning other sins more severely, trouble threatens. One runs the risk of being personally suspected of libertinism and laxity—a risk, incidentally, which even our Saviour did not escape, for the reproach was frequently levelled at Him, "Why doth your master eat with publicans and sinners?" (Matt. 9:11; 11:19; 21:31; Mark 2:16; Luke 5:30; 7:34). In the end it boils down to this: the gospel is our primer not only in dogma and morality, but also in pastoral matters; its contents as well as its methods should determine our procedure. In the Gospels there are comparatively few passages dealing with prostitution; but for every one of them there are dozens referring to hypocrisy and breaches of brotherly love. This alone shows up the Holy Scriptures in pleasing contrast with most compendiums on morality, in which sex usually has a whole section to itself, an honor rarely extended to the more important virtue of love for one's neighbor. Christ, the Good Shepherd (John 10:11), the Bishop of our souls (I Pet. 2:25), castigated no sin so severely as that of uncharitableness. Indeed, He sometimes made use of expressions which are quite frightening. "And whosoever shall say to his brother Raca . . . shall be in danger of hell fire" (Matt. 5:22); "It is easier for a camel to pass through the eye of a needle than for a rich man to enter into the kingdom of heaven" (Matt. 19:24; Mark 10:25; Luke 18:25). These passages show an inexorable severity towards uncharitableness and want of mercy. The shattering condemnation of the Scribes and Pharisees is directed against their hypocrisy, their lack of charity, their greed, their pride—but not one word is said about prostitution. Our Lord's most penetrating illustrations deal with brotherly love: that of the Good Samaritan, the unjust steward, the Pharisee and the publican, and so on. But where in the whole of the gospels do we find a similar sternness shown to the sexual offender? Surely the examples touching this trespass are an absolute proof of our Lord's endless love and mercy. "Go, and now sin no more" (John 8:11); "Many sins are forgiven her, because she hath loved much" (Luke 7:47); "He that is without sin among you, let him first cast a stone at her" (John 8:7). The plea frequently made, that these passages can only refer to particularly repentant sinners, is a risky one because it would pave the way to every inconvenient passage of the Bible being treated as an exception.

It is a strange thing that many promulgators of the gospel feel somewhat embarrassed by the boundless, truly divine compassion which our Lord shows toward sinners and which is an essential characteristic of His nature. It is rather like the attitude of the Prodigal's brother, who simply cannot understand the father's kindness to the erring son. The Scribes and Pharisees of the Old Testament were not the only ones who took exception to this quality. Many narrow, shortsighted natures feel that the kindness of our Lord is somehow pedagogically at fault, and they are inclined to encumber the gospel narratives with many an "if" and a "but"—or to pass them over in the belief that they might encourage lax Christians to throw sexual control to the winds. As long ago as the fourth and fifth centuries, monastic scribes prepared quite a number of manuscript copies of St. John's Gospel leaving out the story of the adulteress (8:1) altogether, in their anxiety as to the effect it might produce. St. Augustine sternly criticizes this sort of proceeding and accuses those who practice it of being weak in their faith ("modicae fidei vel potius inimici verae fidei." *De adulterinis conjugiis* 2. 7; Migne, PL 40, 474). Of course, even St.

Augustine could not prevent these truncated versions from enjoying an extensive circulation long after they were written—nor could he hinder the silent suppression of passages here and there by many a later preacher. If it comes to that, every instance of compassion, every consoling truth, lends itself to distortion if frivolity or calculated ingenuity are bent on misusing it. There will always be a few narrow-minded teachers who, in their pedagogic zeal, prefer the shock tactics of dogmatic vigor to the more gentle methods of compassion and, with the best intentions in the world, avoid anything that might lead to the least relaxation of severity. It never occurs to them that their shortsightedness may throw the whole teaching out of balance, or that their exaggeration and bias may turn the "tidings of great joy" into the very opposite. Is not this the reason why we priests are so often rejected as advisers on moral questions, since we are suspected from the outset of having prejudiced views which make an unbiased approach to such problems impossible?

Nowhere do we find this "schoolmasterly" approach more in evidence than in the case of the Sixth Commandment. There are many, even including serious, thoughtful men, who believe that the danger of sins against chastity cannot be emphasized too much—and that too little emphasis laid upon them is bound to be disastrous. Chastity and morality are concepts that have become so identical in their minds that they are incapable even of noticing exaggerations—or, if they do notice them, they find a ready excuse in the motive, "prevention is better than cure." While they will let even the heresy of Tertullian pass for true coinage, they become highly uncomfortable when the claims of love to priority are rightfully stressed. The objection that this order of precedence "might give license for sexual liberty to the adherents of the new sexual morality" is immediately raised.[1] No teaching and no book—least of all the Book of Books—is safe from misuse by those whose intentions are evil. But the truth of the primacy of love is registered on hundreds of pages of the Holy Scriptures and is stressed so emphatically that it cannot be overlooked, and should certainly not be suppressed in modern writings and sermons.

Perhaps one of the worst consequences, however, of a pedagogic system that edits the gospel *in usum Delphini,* and makes this abridged version the sole arbiter of Christian morality, is that it tends to brand the true order of values in the moral sphere with the taint of laxity. Instead of regulating their teachings by the clear and definite ruling of the Scriptures, these pedagogues deem it wiser to set sins against chastity above those against love, out of fear that they might be underrated. The still greater risk that sins against charity might be assessed too lightly gives them no concern—as if the word "lax" could apply to nothing but sex. They overlook the fact that their well-meant pedagogy is leading them from the Scylla of sexual license to the Charybdis of a still greater laxity, namely, to an unwarrantably lenient view of the worst trespass of all, the sin against love. By focusing the attention of conscientious Christians too sharply on the Sixth Commandment, they push the claims of love completely into the background. Thus, they bring up the young to a kind of morality that will "strain out a gnat and swallow a camel" (Matt. 23: 24)—that, for fear of the least false step in sexual life, will let the far worse sins of unforgiveness, greed, ruthlessness, and so on appear quite negligible. As one modern author quite rightly says: "The moral theologians say there is no *parvitas materiae in sexto*—that is to say, all sins are equal and all grievous; but there appears to be no *gravitas materiae* in sins against love nowadays. They can all be treated lightly." [2]

It should hardly be necessary to prove that there is no shortage of laxity in regard to sins against love. The teachings of the Catholic Church on faith and morality constitute a unified structure in which every beam and stone has its appointed place and its own specific function within the framework of the whole. All are necessary; not one can afford to be shifted without undue strain. Every exaggeration of one truth must therefore be made at the expense of another. In the end, the system which indulges in such overemphasis must come to grief on its own ground, for the very aim it pursues with so much determination proves false and unworkable. According to Thomas Aquinas, whose teachings are shared by the whole Church, love is the "form" of all other virtues. That means that all other potential virtues are embraced in charity; hence chastity, properly understood, also proceeds out of love—but never the other way about. If, on the other hand, the principal virtue is undervalued, all that follows from it will also suffer. A morality that pays less attention to inner sinfulness than to outward honor, that values public opinion and therefore probably elevates self-righteousness and rumor to the seat of judgment, may make an outward show of superior strictness, but actually it will scarcely avoid shamelessness. It will lead to unhealthy prudery on the one hand and to unnatural perversion on the other, as the history of the sexual question has already proved on so many occasions. And what is it that suffers from all this? Not only love, and honesty, justice, and truth, but also chastity.

On the same grounds, it may be said that sins against the Sixth Commandment receive a quite disproportionate amount of attention in the confessional, especially in comparison with sins against brotherly love. It is quite wrong, as Alphonsus [3] points out, that sins against chastity should present the richest and most abundant material for confession (*frequentior atque abundantior confessionum materia*). Many pious people believe it their duty to examine and accuse themselves far more in connection with the Sixth Commandment than with any other. Eighty per cent of these scrupulous folk, who for the most part are responsible and conscientious, live in a perpetual state of anxiety on this point. It can also happen that less conscientious penitents work themselves up into a highly excited state over some small, imaginary lapse in this connection, while passing over with complete indifference a ruthless disregard of family obligations, an unloving, inconsiderate disposition, and a tendency to unkind judgment. Naturally, every priest tries to keep strictly to the recommendation to ask too little rather than too much in such cases; but, unconsciously, the scrupulous confessor will fall into the habit of paying greater attention to the sin which is so often presented to him as the most heinous of all crimes.

Anxiety is aroused most of all through the custom, which constantly recurs in every sermon course and which rests on the authority of St. Alphonsus, of representing unchastity as the sin through which the majority of souls are condemned to eternal damnation. This saint writes in *De sexto,* no. 413, that the majority of souls (*major animarum numerus*) go to hell because of sins against chastity; indeed he "has no doubt that most souls are damned through this shameless sin, or at least are not damned without having committed it." Most preachers quote this on the authority of St. Alphonsus; very few fail to avail themselves of his powerful rhetoric. Thus Busl writes (II, 648) : "This is the crime that populates hell. Apart from children dying in innocence, one holy father says, very few adults are saved—and this, all because of sins against chastity." Similarly, if not quite so crudely, Zollner, Wermelskirchen, von Doss, Gatterer, and many others use the same material. Unfortunately, one of the latest recruits to this viewpoint is Tihamer Toth,[4] who adds the exaggeration: "Ninety-nine out of every hundred are damned solely for this sin."

It would be interesting to trace the origin of this thought back to the source from which St. Alphonsus derived it. But that would require a full-length study on its own. Anyone who wishes to explore the subject will have to carry his researches right back to the very earliest centuries of Christianity, where he will doubtless find some clues in Neoplatonic-Manichean teaching. It may even be that the impression owes its first impetus to some chance remark of the great bishop of Hippo whose early works are notorious for the occasional bubbles of his earlier Manichean convictions that keep coming up in them. It would not be the first time that a great man's influence has come down through the ages, not only through his most valuable works, but, accidentally, through some side issues for which he may not even be responsible; for many of these ideas slipped in through the overenthusiasm of disciples who fathered them onto their teacher and passed on this garbled version of his views to posterity. In his *Sermo* 250, cap. 2, the bishop of Hippo lets fall the quite general observation that: "Among all the battles a Christian has to wage, the toughest of all is that against unchastity; here there is daily struggle, and only rare victory." The clue becomes a little clearer when we arrive at Isidor of Seville (*De summo bono* II, 39). Isidor carries the thought a little further by saying: "The Devil put more human beings under his yoke through unchasity than through any other sin." This saint, who died in 636, is, after Augustine and Gregory, one of the most read authors of the Middle Ages, although the literary merit of his works falls far behind that of these other great teachers. It may be that he is the actual originator of this teaching. At all events, the very general views of Augustine receive at his hands a much more pointed, not to say overdone, emphasis. But all the same, such views do not become glaringly obvious until some hundreds of years later. Thomas cites the passage from Isidor in his *Summa Theologica* (2-2, q. 154, a. 3, ad 1), but only to render it more innocuous. He uses it as an illustration of the ease with which the violence of sensual passion can bring about a man's downfall, pointing out, however, that the resulting check on will power rather minimizes the guilt of the sin than intensifies it. Thomas, in common with his contemporaries, values the pronouncements of the fathers far too highly to contradict them; but he bends them more or less arbitrarily to fit into his own system, and this quotation is a typical example of his method. In its later and more drastic form, we come upon this idea (perhaps for the first time?) among the works of the celebrated Franciscan teacher, Dietrich von Koelde: "Unchastity is the greatest enemy of the soul. You should know, that for this sin alone, condemnation falls on the majority of mankind."[5] It was only through Alphonsus that this teaching gained universal circulation, not among theologians, but among preachers and ascetics. But not even the universally recognized authority of this teacher of the Church has yet resulted in its being incorporated in any textbook on dogma or in any treatise on moral theology. If it has succeeded in establishing itself firmly in pulpit oratory, the reason is to be sought not in its dogmatic soundness, but in its presumed effectiveness as a rhetorical figure.

All the above-mentioned preachers who press it into service to show up the iniquity of prostitution in the most glaring colors quote Alphonsus as their authority. Not one of them makes any attempt to put it on a dogmatic basis, with the sole exception of Hunolt. And Hunolt, who borrowed the idea not from his contemporary, Alphonsus, but from the French court preachers of the rococo period, commits the almost unbelievable error of making one of his authorities the recognized Montanist, Tertullian, whose polemical attacks against the authority of the Church had led to his eventual defection.

The opinion of Alphonsus is, therefore, not endorsed by any legitimate tradition and appears to come from some doubtful, not to say sinister, sources. There is no solid basis for it, either in the Scriptures or in teachings of the fathers; rather the reverse. If there were any justifiable foundation for the idea that the great majority of mankind are eternally damned because of this sin, the mildness our Lord showed in relation to it would be inexplicable. In His judgment concerning the damned (Matt. 25:41), He does not even mention this most debatable of all sins—He speaks only of crimes against charity. And the fathers and theologians devote comparatively little attention to this class of sin, in contrast with others, although it is said to have such a vital importance for the eternal salvation of man. Dogmaticians might also be justified in asking where Alphonsus got hold of this knowledge which he retails so boldly. How could he know the exact proportion of souls condemned for this fault? All the practical experience which a bishop or a specialist in the cure of souls might have at his command would be insufficient as a basis of calculation. A very definite divine revelation would have been necessary to justify such an unqualified pronouncement on the ultimate fate of millions and millions of sinners. But universally recognized revelation is silent on this point; therefore, it could only rest upon some private revelation, of which there is neither proof nor evidence. As this opinion of his also appeared quite late in the day, and is totally unknown to the early teaching of the Church, there can be no question of *consensus theologorum* either. So this must surely be a case where one is fully justified in differing from the opinion of an isolated teacher on the important grounds already stated —a freedom which all theologians may permit themselves, even with regard to authorities like Augustine or Thomas. With all due respect to Alphonsus, it appears that there is a teaching which requires much more thorough investigation before it can be justly accepted. Quite apart from the fact that it makes the fear motive a decisive factor in moral endeavor, the use of this teaching probably shares with the *parvitas materiae* clause the responsibility for spreading, both among the clergy and the general public, the notion that unchastity is a sin altogether different and more grievous than any other sin—a notion which is now taken to represent the essence of morality.

Another statement which crops up repeatedly in sermons since Hunolt's day is that which singles out offenses against chastity as the most dangerous because they are incurable. "Unchastity is an offense that makes conversion difficult, in fact, almost impossible"; Bourdaloue calls it "plus irremissible." As already mentioned, both Bernard and Thomas take the opposite view. They teach, on the contrary, that sins of the spirit, like pride and avarice, are far more dangerous than sins of the flesh because they bury themselves in man's nature more insidiously and, for this very reason, man has more difficulty in detecting them.[6] Brother Berthold of Ratisbon is of the same opinion. He considers that the sin which sends most people to hell is disloyalty, under which heading he naturally embraces a whole host of trespasses, such as greed, usury, cheating, hypocrisy, lukewarmness. But, in Brother Berthold's opinion, the most unforgivable sin is avarice—"the most devilish of them all." "The unchaste do give God a little peace now and then," he says, "by ceasing from their sin; but the avaricious are forever wrapt up in their gold, they give God no thought at all, and whatever I may say to them is wasted, for they never dream of repenting." In the nineteenth sermon on the Ten Commandments of our Lord, he says: "I must devote half my sermon once again to you [O, avaricious one!] and still I know that it will do no good." [7]

It is surely no mere coincidence that all the sinners mentioned in the gospels as being repentant and ready to atone (Luke 7:47; John 8:7; 8:11) are, without exception, those who have offenses against chastity on their conscience—never those guilty of violating love, like the spiteful and self-righteous Pharisees who are so often reproved by our Saviour for their unwillingness to repent. "Amen I say to you, that the publicans and the harlots shall go into the kingdom of God before you" (Matt. 21:31. See also the whole of chapter 23). As already mentioned, the early fathers also often speak of Christians who lead chaste lives but are lacking in love. Augustine gives a warning against this "sterile virginity," while Bernard likens it to a lamp without oil. And surely every priest has made the discovery that it is easier to bring an unchaste sinner to see the error of his ways and mend them, temporarily at least, than to make a miserly or an unforgiving person even admit his fault.

The unchaste person's resistance to conversion is a thing that needs proving. It is the very nature of things that sins of the spirit should be more deep-seated and much more a part of man's character than sins of the flesh. The former are permanently rooted, whereas the sins of the unchaste "do give God a little peace now and then." Experience teaches us that sins like pride or unforgiveness can be so much a part of a man's nature that he is completely unaware of them. In a naturally proud or egoistical person, they are far more difficult to deal with than the sins of the flesh in an easygoing, unchaste sinner. It not infrequently happens that such a person is sufficiently noble by nature to suffer inwardly at the very thought of his weakness—such natures are often ready and waiting for grace, which is not infrequently awakened in them by the understanding words of a wise and kindhearted confessor. As has already been mentioned above, the lives of many of the saints prove how the light of grace may illumine the soul and turn those who previously had been completely given over to the pleasures of the flesh into devout and saintly Christians. The bishop of Hippo gives many examples of such conversion, and is one of the chief witnesses for the defense of repentant sinners who have offended against chastity. Rarely, if ever, can we find among the legends of the saints a single instance of a miser or an egoist being converted.

Because of the uncompromising severity with which many preachers treat offenses against chastity, a feeling of depression and uselessness is often engendered, and this can lead to an inner rebellion. The thought, "Oh, what is the use? I am no good anyway," robs many of the last remnants of shame and whatever sense of honor they may have retained. Certainly, chastity requires the utmost attention, especially in the instruction of the young; but the best ends are by no means served by a constant reiteration of grim warnings. This is more likely to stir the imagination and induce an unhealthy preoccupation with sexual guilt. It is perfectly right, of course, to point out to young people that unchastity saps the strength of both soul and body, making weaklings and slaves of its victims and enervating them before they have arrived at their best—also that it destroys all natural resilience, dispels joy, trust in God, consolation in prayer, and self-dependence. It destroys that child-likeness which God expects even from adults (Matt. 18: 3). Even poets recognize the beauty of that pure child-likeness. Did not Heinrich Heine write?:

> You are like a flower, so noble, fine and pure—
> I look at you, and a wave of deep emotion
> Catches at my heart.

But the instructor should never miss an opportunity of pointing out that the unchaste man need not necessarily be the very worst sinner. He is one who should be more pitied than condemned. The instructor will fare far better if he models himself on the gentleness of our Saviour in relation to the unchaste, than if he takes dogmatically false expressions such as "the greatest and most devastating of all sins" as his pattern.

One ought to guard against using drastic and exaggerated phraseology in dealing with sex life. Words like "bestial" ought to be cut out altogether. We quite rightly condemn the apostles of the shameless Age of Enlightenment for degrading man in sexual matters to the level of animals; but we ought to guard against using the same kind of language ourselves. Man shares not only the sex instinct with animals, but the physical as a whole—the total organic and sensitive system. It happens to be the will of the Creator that the survival of the race should depend on the same principle of propagation throughout the whole of animate life. Anyone who regards this as degrading is unconsciously subscribing to Manichean ideas. The whole question of sexual enlightenment has only become involved because religious thinking, leaning too much to a one-sided, spiritual viewpoint, has fallen into the habit of regarding the mystery of sex life as in some way dishonorable. That is why a great many highly moral and sensitive natures cannot rid themselves of the notion that sex is somehow "impure," and that we should be far better without it, since it is too much inclined to drag the spiritual side of man's nature down to the level of the sensual.

And yet a great deal that is positive and ideal can be drawn from these proofs. How much exaltation there is in the very thought that God creates souls, but leaves the forming of the actual physical body to the parents of the new life! The way in which the love of two persons calls another life into being brings to mind the flower-spangled meadows springing from the lap of the earth under the kiss of the sun; the way the young child, lying under the heart of its mother, draws its flesh from her flesh, its blood from her blood; the strong tie of natural love that binds the young life into closest unity with that of its parents; and the fact that it is not only physically but also spiritually a wonderful reproduction of father and mother—all these thoughts do make us realize the boundless wisdom and bounty of God who ordered all things in this fashion. The author has often proved that even the most frivolous young people are deeply impressed when they can be brought to realize that they already carry within themselves that future life for whose physical and spiritual heritage here on earth they are responsible, since what they hand on to their children will depend upon themselves. When a preacher or a teacher, in an excess of zeal, lumps the whole erotic impulse into one common trespass with the label "bestial," surely he is almost forcing young people to look at these things in their most unworthy light, and branding them as unclean without the slightest discrimination. How many a young person, thanks to this kind of instruction, has been unable to rid himself for the remainder of his existence of the idea that there is something degrading about the whole of sex life!

In the Holy Scriptures, uncompromising as they are on trespasses against chastity and on unnatural perversions, a dignified, positive attitude is always brought to bear on sex matters. The most striking example is the Song of Songs, in which bridal love is depicted in very concrete images as the symbol of supernatural love. If true believers and good Catholics, unlike the early mystics, are unable to bring a real appreciation to this book, much as they respect the Scriptures—and not forgetting that it is included in the canon of the Church—the reason must be sought not least in the low estimate of "sensual" love which is nowadays almost universal. And yet, even in this example, we see how the New Testament preserves the germ of the Old, and how the Old only arrives at its full significance in the light of the New. The bridal mysticism, which the Song of Songs illustrates with such sharply etched vignettes, runs through the whole mentality of the Old Testament, in which Jehovah's relationship with His people is depicted as a bridal or marital one, just as apostasy from Him is regarded as equal to the breaking of marriage vows (Isai. 54:5; 62:5; Os. 2:19, and so on). Our Lord takes up the same picture and describes Himself repeatedly as the "bridegroom" of His Church (Matt. 9:15; 25:6; Mark 2:19; Luke 5:34). St. John the Baptist called himself (John 3:29) "the friend of the Bridegroom," and describes his joy at the appearance of the Messiah with the happiness which the friends of the bridegroom detect in his voice when he cries out with joy on greeting the bride. St. Paul, too, takes up the simile (II Cor. 11:2; Eph. 5:32) and compares the union of married people with the blessed communion of Christ and His Church. The same apostle speaks in an unembarrassed, factual way about the duties of the married state and ennobles them through this sacred comparison. The mysticism of the Middle Ages expresses the same thoughts in charming though often naïve pictures. If present-day sexual psychologists of the Freudian school see [8] in this bridal mysticism only a misuse of religion for purposes similar to the temple prostitution of olden days, that surely is a tasteless misunderstanding of the most profound message of these comparisons. It might be more permissible to suggest that there is a certain similarity between them and the Greek mysticism of Amor and Psyche, of the interplay of earthly, intellectual, and divine elements, or, in other words, love that has been raised to a spiritual level. But dare we reproach those outside the fold with their errors, when such inspiring images have become strangers to our own thought world, largely because of our shyness in all sexual matters? Nowadays, no preacher would dare to compare the radiant dawn with a bridegroom's joy on entering the bridal chamber (Ps. 18:6), or to speak of the rights and duties of married life in the intimate words used by St. Paul (I Cor. 7), or in the language used by his admirer, St. John Chrysostom, in a public sermon on the same subject. The latter example is particularly important because, in it, the great preacher condemns as heretical (i.e., Manichean) the qualms which would look askance at such plain speaking: "They shall be two in one flesh—that results from the coition; it mingles the two bodies making them one substance. It is the same thing that happens when oil is added to an unguent. Why should you be ashamed of that which is not dishonorable? Why blush at something which is perfectly pure? Leave that to heretics. My purpose is to show marriage in all its purity, to restore it to its original honor and to shut the mouths of heretics." [9] The same saint also compares the desire for Holy Communion with the longing an infant displays at its mother's breast (*Hom. 60 ad populum*). The simple and natural way in which sexual matters were treated by the nun-poetess Hroswitha of Gandersheim and by the great St. Hildegard has already been mentioned, and the same frankness in medieval art, in prayers, customs, and teachings gave rise to no embarrassment even though it took forms and mentioned things which nowadays would greatly shock, not only a few ultra-sensitive people, but the public as a whole. In some districts of Old Bavaria, each *Ave* of the Angelus is succeeded by the charming words: "Blessed the womb that bore Thee, blessed the breasts that gave Thee suck." If this prayer, literally taken from the Scriptures, were to be generally reintroduced, it would be almost certain to call forth protests from large numbers of the faithful—their sensibilities are too easily offended. Does not the erstwhile Old Catholic pastor, K. Jentsch,[10] state that the majority of his parishoners rejected the "Hail, Mary" because they could not send their wives and children to a service in which "the fruit of the womb" was mentioned? And these objectors were men of standing, accustomed in their private gatherings with male companions to show none of the moral tenderness of which they boasted in public. But have we not all degenerated into adopting a somewhat prudish tone when we refer to things as unfit to be spoken of, although they are God-created and have a definite part to play in the fulfillment of the divine will? Our very embarrassment has an exaggerated quality which should warn us that it is not quite genuine. Pictures our devout forefathers venerated because of the piety they inspired are nowadays stowed away because we are too "moral" to look at them. Folk songs and even biblical texts are blue-penciled, but it does not seem to occur to those who are so anxious about morals that this very anxiety betrays lack of confidence, just as prudery is very often a pharisaical mantle hiding deception and lust. In Catholic lands of southern Europe, where Puritanism and the "enlightenment" of the early nineteenth century gained no firm foothold, one may even today come across folk customs and simple, unembarrassed forms of speech which were accepted just as unquestionably in Germany before the Reformation. Italians can see no harm whatever in a mother feeding her infant at the breast in public; but if this happened among more cold-blooded northern people, the police would step in on the grounds of morality. Yet it quite often happens that the peasant women who attend to their maternal duties while resting on church benches or in public places are modestly dressed and indulge in none of those refined arts of allurement which women of "better" class society understand to perfection. Prudery is substituted for chastity; and that natural behavior which is, in fact, the essence of chastity, is scornfully rejected.

Of course, it must not be supposed that this book, in advocating natural behavior, supports that naturalism which, for instance, maintains that sexual matters should be treated with the same inconsequence as eating and drinking. Naturally, the former will always demand a certain reserve. Decent shame, which guards these intimate matters, is as old as mankind; it is not just a contracted habit or "a rudimentary remnant of bygone, dark ages." [11] It is a person's natural protection against the violence of sexual passion. God gave man this instinct and added lust as a great incentive for the maintenance of the species. If the sense of shame did not keep lust in check, mankind would be devoured by it. Whereas in the case of animals the instinct is regulated more or less automatically, since it only functions at certain periods, man has reason and will and can choose his own course; and he has the precious gift of shame to keep watch and ward over his proceedings. One of the foremost duties of good upbringing is to foster this sense of shame, the "stout fortress of good morals," as Wolfram von Eschenbach calls it. Once the sense of shame vanishes, the flood gates are open, and man's nature is submerged in lust and depravity. But some instructors make the grave mistake of imagining that shame gains in effectiveness in proportion to the contempt it brings to bear on sex. Shame and the sexual urge are two opposites which can both be accentuated; shame can degenerate into prudery, and the sexual urge to shameless license. It is obvious, therefore, that the solution does not lie in the greatest possible augmentation of shame. It consists of a clear and definite recognition of the border line between that which is sinful and impure in regard to sex and that which, in accordance with God's will, seems right and necessary. Imagination, acting upon the erotic impulse, spreads a delicate, holy veil over the mysteries of sex life. "Mystery is not hypocrisy; a race dies out, when it loses all sense of shame" (Th. Vischer). But this proper shame does not build artificial, unnatural walls around the functions of the sexual instinct and declare them to be impure. An unhealthy overdevelopment of the sense of shame may lead, in one person, to inhibitions and excessive scruples and, in another, to a violent recoil, ending in the destruction of all inner standards.

The best kind of upbringing, therefore, is not one which keeps young people in ignorance as long as possible and removes from their attention everything that might excite their curiosity on sexual matters. The young should be accustomed to look at things with pure eyes, and to judge them accordingly. Shame does not mean fear of the naked body; it trusts the body reverently. How well the Apostle brings out this reverence in his admonition on chastity! "Fly fornication . . . Or know you not that your members are the temple of the Holy Ghost, who is in you, whom you have from God: and you are not your own? For you are bought with a great price. Glorify and bear God in your body." (I Cor. 6:18).

It is not the man who ignores sex, as if it were beneath him, who is most chaste; it is the man who recognizes his body for what it is, and can look at it with eyes that are pure. In this connection, grave errors have been made by pedagogues of the past—not excluding Catholic ones—and all with the very best of motives. In the sexual education of youth, as in pronouncements from the pulpit, a puritanical zeal led to the radical course being invariably regarded as the best. Here the Judaical maxim: "Touch not. Taste not. Handle not" (Col. 2:21) became the cornerstone of ideal sexual pedagogy. Because there were unchaste dances, dancing was entirely forbidden; because there were improper theaters and films, people were told it was better for pious Christians not to patronize the opera or the movies; because some works of art were obscene, even mature young people were forbidden to go to art galleries. Walls were erected to shut out evil—but these were no more a proof of genuine modesty than locks and bolts are a proof of honesty. The classics were expurgated; folk songs were mutilated and robbed of all that simplicity which gave them their unique charm; there were even some overzealous instructors who laid impious hands on the Scriptures themselves with a view to "improving" them, and pains were taken to delete passages which might draw undue attention to sexual matters when expounding the Bible to young people—as if these very passages, in their direct and unexceptionable simplicity, were not aids which earnest teachers could profitably employ in putting over a pure and adequate concept of sexual morality. Naturally, it was thought that chastity and modesty could be best served by pretending that the erotic element simply did not exist; but these zealots overlooked the fact that when young people, after being boxed up for years in cotton wool screening, suddenly overthrow this screen and plunge headlong into real life, they not only find to their dismay that sex certainly does exist, but that it has a way of making its existence most imperatively felt. Can one wonder that, after so much mollycoddling, many of the young are quite unprepared to cope with this imperative insistence? Whether we like it or not, sex is a fact and, moreover, one created by God in accordance with His holy will. Of course, man need not be a slave to it. It can be kept under control, it can be diverted, but it cannot be ignored or uprooted. Where it is not mastered from within and replaced by a stronger impulse—where it is merely concealed from young people by outward means—it will seek a sudden vent of its own for its destructive force, and the ultimate violence of its destructive power will be greater in proportion to the unnatural restraint previously put upon it. The bigoted bias which leads so many instructors of the young to emphasize the spiritual and supernatural qualities in the human make-up too much, entirely ignoring the claims of physical man, can lead to real catastrophe. "We often strive to become pure angels, and in doing so fail to become good men," says St. Francis de Sales.

The young man who has been brought up to an unself-conscious, blameless intercourse with the opposite sex—to the kind of conduct which is the essence of pure knighthood and nobility—will be in all ways better armored to withstand the temptation of sexual instinct than one who has been too carefully sheltered and kept from a knowledge of the facts of life. One who can look upon the naked body, when necessary, without feeling at all uncomfortable is actually more modest than one who has been accustomed to be shocked at nakedness. And if we recognize this truth, all the antagonism that so often exists in the attitude of the oversensitive to pure art will quickly vanish. Man is made in the image of God, and even in his body incorporates the highest idea of created beauty; so we cannot blame the artist if he tries to capture on canvas or in carving a reconstruction of that beauty. True art consists in the ability to display all that is æsthetic in the naked body without calling undue attention to its erotic aspect. A young person should be taught to distinguish between the pure art of a Michelangelo or a Dürer and those examples of painting and sculpture which appeal only to the lowest instincts.[12] The sinister influences which are forever at work to deprave young people, through the medium of films, cheap literature, questionable sports, and comics widely circulated (often privately), cannot be fought by mere negation. It is good to know that Church and state are actively cooperating in campaigns to clean up the amusement fare of the young and that many modern artists are coming back to the view that art is truly the "daughter of religion."

The question, "How shall I tell my child?" has grown

out of the radical attitude which Puritan influences brought to bear upon the Sixth Commandment, and which has gradually become general.

Serious, conscientious, and religious parents are often more shy than others in approaching this question, precisely because their very refinement leads them to take the more "spiritual" attitude, with the result that any reference to purely physical and sexual needs creates embarrassment and humiliation. Our ancestors regarded these matters with far more simplicity and natural modesty. Therefore, the question never presented any difficulty. Naturally, we Catholics reject most emphatically anything that would weaken the inherent safeguard of modest shame. But at the same time, any well-meant "skating over thin ice," any attempt to hedge, must be condemned as ill-advised. The air of particularly pompous solemnity which so often accompanies a first explanation of the facts of life—especially when it bursts on the youngster out of the blue after a carefully maintained secrecy on the matter—is bound to convey the impression that there is something just a little indecent about this extraordinary arrangement of nature. Even in the best of circumstances, a sudden revelation made in this way is bound to start a child's imagination working and this may bring a whole host of other dangers in its train. Here we can once again take a lesson from our forefathers, who made no such mystery of the processes of nature, so that children became familiar with the mention of them from their earliest age. Children in those days knew nothing about the solemnity of a "special session for enlightenment"—still less were their ideas confused by silly stories like the stork legend. They absorbed the necessary information quite naturally, stage by stage, usually in the form of prayers and religious instruction, so that, when they arrived at full understanding, they never quite realized when the knowledge had first begun to dawn upon them. And why should not the youngest child learn that its life began under the heart of its mother, and that it is indebted for its existence to both its parents? Fortified with this knowledge even before it goes to school, where it may possibly come into contact with bad companions, it is much less likely to be contaminated than the child that has been carefully "sheltered" from all natural knowledge because of the squeamishness of its over-refined family.

The best kind of sexual education is not that which perpetually draws attention to the dangers of unchastity, or even that which is fond of preaching chastity as the most important virtue. Indirect education is always more effective. The wise instructor will not attempt to lead the young to love through chastity, but the other way about—to chastity through love. He will not encourage the conscientious child, in the confessional and in examination of conscience, to dwell inordinately on this one point—like a bird fascinated by a snake. He will strive to follow in the footsteps of the Divine Teacher who, with the most exquisite sensibility, touched upon the Sixth Commandment only in passing, as it were, and devoted the primary force of His pastoral teaching to promulgating the doctrine of love, to which He referred again and again. He will stress the spirit of love in his religious instruction—that genuine, pious comradeship, that knightly conduct toward the opposite sex which keeps more pernicious notions at bay. He will keep well in the foreground among supernatural aids the powerful protection of frequent Holy Communion—"the warm hearth of God's love," as the author of *The Imitation of Christ* calls it—and, when dealing with true penitents, will not, in the confessional, try to rouse too much anxiety on the subject of sex. It might even be an encouragement to young people to suggest that they should come as often as possible to Communion in the knowledge that they are free from sin and do not require the sacrament of penance. If the instructor succeeds in diverting a youth from sexual peril by inducing him to fix his whole attention, through love, on a higher ideal, he has the satisfaction of having given his pupil a greater resistance to future temptation from his erotic impulses. Such indirect approaches to chastity are far more effective and more lasting in their result than perpetual warnings on the risks this virtue runs. Love is the warm glow that develops in the young heart the necessary power to formulate ideals; it is also the source of energy that, with God's help, enables him to attain them. It "beareth all things, believeth all things, hopeth all things" (I Cor. 13:7), "for it never falleth away." Chastity is awakened by love; but the contrary is never true. How very mistaken is the system of education that mixes these two as cause and effect—that leaves the true source of strength untapped, offering mankind in exchange a homemade substitute which requires all kinds of mental jugglery to make it reasonable! All the fine sentiments and lofty phrases in the world are of no avail when the resistance, built up by long and patient effort of will, is suddenly swept aside by overwhelming passion. Will without principles grounded in a true chastity, which has become second nature, can prove so very weak! Therein lies the tragedy of many a young soul, even though it be religiously inclined. But the moment a young person becomes absorbed in a genuine ideal, accepted with love and lovingly cherished, he can no longer be deceived by false values, however alluringly his imagination may conjure them up. It should always be the primary task of religious instruction to plant such ideals in young souls, thereby diverting the attention from sexual matters instead of constantly painting the dangers from this source in the most lurid colors. And, in the formative years, a genuine affection for some high-principled, good girl may yet save many a young man when the devil has already begun to draw him into his maelstrom. It would not be the first time God has caused the withered staff of a modern young Tannhäuser to blossom, thus confounding one of His own representatives who, in an excess of zeal, felt himself justified in pronouncing the sentence of damnation.

Sometimes the severe standard applied to sexual behavior nowadays is excused on the ground that we have more licentiousness to cope with today than ever our ancestors knew. It is quite true that, in this present age, we are caught up in circumstances which were brought about by the highly materialistic views which dominated all thinking for more than a century. Many of the barriers handed down through old-established traditions kept hot-blooded young people under stricter control and put a brake on free intercourse between the sexes—but these have now been swept aside. An entirely new way of life has set in. When grandfather courted grandmother, their meetings were still to a large extent chaperoned. Public opinion demanded that young ladies, at any rate, should be most carefully guarded. Today these artificial limitations no longer exist. Dances and theater parties, outings, and weekend trips enable comrades of both sexes to meet without the slightest restriction, and no young person thinks this kind of companionship is wrong.

Some of their elders are not quite so sanguine; but, all the same, one should guard against comparisons which show up the black spots of modern custom too sharply in contrast with the supposedly golden age of the past.

Certainly the innocence of youth is nowadays far more a matter of individual responsibility. The young folk have to square up their behavior with their own conscience. But there have in every age been grievous offenses against the Sixth Commandment—history tells us of periods when chastity was far less esteemed than it is even in our own time. The pictures painted by, for instance, Salvian in the fifth century, Ratherius of Verona or Peter Damian in the eighth and tenth centuries, Geiler von Kaysersberg in the fifteenth century, and so on, warn us against the haste with which many preachers jump to the conclusion that no age is more fit to be castigated from the pulpit than their own. And if we extend the concept of morality beyond the mere question of sex to a broader universal basis, the comparison of our own time with that unhappy period when witch-mania appeared to have the whole of humanity in its grip must give rise to deeper reflections. We need, in this connection, only read the descriptions given by von Spee in his *Cautio criminalis.* Writing from personal observation of the excesses to which this mania led, he lashes the mob, the lust for power shown by many lawyers, and the fanaticism of a section of the clergy mercilessly. Taking all this into account, we should be very chary of hankering after the "good old times." Nearly all preachers of morals treat their own period as if it were the worst ever; even the good Berthold of Ratisbon, the greatest pulpit orator of a period which is looked upon as the flowering of the Middle Ages in its deeply devout Catholicism, laments that the youth of his day seems to be backsliding. "Nowadays the chicks have scarcely emerged from the shell before they claim their liberty to be unchaste." [13] A *laudator temporis acti*—one who extols the past—will no doubt always find support among the older generation. Critical moral word-pictures give the speaker a better chance to display his brilliance than factual delineations of the faith. Yet it would sometimes be more rewarding to bring a positive attitude into play, pointing out the better way to young people, instead of merely holding up their faults for reprimand. There is no need always to lay the finger on gaping wounds; in all periods there are sublime and beautiful things, too, that demand our admiration. Unless all the signs deceive, it is precisely our own age which is faced with the task of emphasizing the Christian ideal of universal brotherhood and equality, of social justice, so that these may be extended to the ends of the earth and leave their imprint on humanity for all time. This ideal cannot be furthered by denial alone. The call of the Holy Father for Catholic Action—that is, for positive cooperation—is more than an appeal to various unions to redouble their respective efforts. It is our duty to listen to the inner voice of God instead of hanging on the words of momentarily fashionable critics or, at least, being content to pour new wine into old bottles. Today our most important duty is to direct the attention of youth to the tasks that face it —tasks which will have a fateful effect upon future generations. We Catholics enjoy the inestimable advantage of having fundamental principles we need not quarrel about. But, precisely for this reason, it is our high duty to make these Catholic truths visible—by incorporating them in our public life, in our family life, and the life of our own community. In order to do this, we must inspire our young people with a real enthusiasm for these principles. There is no greater mistake than that of continually harking back to the past with all its so-called "better times" and those solid safeguards which, we suppose, made people less liable to temptation, while the present, with all its wonderful possibilities, is neglected, quite unjustly and unforgivably. "Whatever is necessary in any period of time is the will of God" (Th. Florentini).

Surely the Holy Ghost is present in His Holy Church no less in this twentieth century than in the bygone days of St. Boniface and St. Francis Xavier. And the spirit of holiness, of faith, of indestructible purity, lives on in "the community of saints" just as truly as it did a thousand years ago. Why should the eyes of the faithful prefer to rest on shadows rather than on the bright glory of present truth? In our work at beds of sickness, in schools, and in various charitable endeavors, we certainly see the darker side of life—but are there not consolations, many examples of true Christianity and quiet heroism? Proofs abound that there are still Christians, men and women who do not "let the left hand know what the right hand doeth"; proof that there are still living martyrs, ready in sickness and suffering to surrender their own will patiently to the will of God, or who, in the most trying circumstances, are ready heroically and conscientiously to serve God in menial offices; that there are still virgins who keep the lily-white banner of purity flying amid the flood of frivolity and lust; still widows whose blameless lives stand comparison with Anna's and Tabitha's, so touchingly referred to in the Scriptures. Decidedly, the Holy Ghost still lives in His Church; we may not always be aware of this if we seek the evidence in imposing gusts and noisy thunder, but the tiny, almost imperceptible breezes will whisper the truth to our hearts. Why in heaven's name do we not preach this more often, so that faithful souls may be filled with love for the Church and, even in the darkest hours, draw a little comfort from it? There is no sense whatever in presenting our own times perpetually as the worst ever; the results can only lead to aggravation of despondent moods, pessimism, and an inferiority complex, even in those who are genuinely sincere in their religion.

Evil is always deceptive. It is part of its very nature to make a better outward impression or, at any rate, more noise than good. The noblest and most selfless virtues are practiced in secret and in silence. Vices either pose as their opposite or cause a scandal; in either case, they are rarely overlooked for want of publicity. Almost every day we hear of disasters, suicides, crimes—and yet ordinary work goes on. We read a great deal about robberies, fraud, and so on—but honesty is so much more common that no one bothers to write about the millions who go on struggling through life, somehow making ends meet and defrauding no one. A great deal is said about broken marriages and tragedies that cause a lot of excitement, but all the time the majority of marriages are happy, or at least normal, and run their course, giving rise to no gossip. And because of all the public clamor about the wrong sort of things, a superficial observer of events might get the impression that the world is full of pitfalls and dangers which no one can escape—a picture which, when you examine it more deeply, is of course entirely false. But because of this biased view, many people allow themselves to become pessimistic. And if Christians hear nothing but the wickedness of the world preached from their pulpits on Sundays, what can one expect? Hopelessness eats its way into the hearts of even the best-intentioned, and it can easily lead to no one having any further belief in ideals. More than ever before, it is the duty of the preacher not only to guard himself against pessimism but, with the help of grace and the power of faith, to overcome all these adverse elements which might awaken it in the hearts of his hearers. "Comfort, comfort my people," says the prophet Isaias (Isai. 40:1); and perhaps never were his words more apt than they are today. The same can be said of the Apostle's admonition: "Comfort the feeble-minded; support the weak; be patient towards all men" (I Thess. 5:14).

This attitude of compassion might well lead to a reassessment, not only of sexual sins, but also of offenders against chastity. This in noway means that the priest should depart from his own strict standard or take the matter otherwise than seriously; but it does mean that he should remember this sin is tied up with all sorts of physical inclinations and material conditions. While most other sins do violence to the spirit—sins like pride, antagonism, egoism, and so on—this particular offense is above all *peccatum carnale,* the sin of the flesh, essentially a sin of weakness rather than downright evil. Furthermore, these sins, as Bishop Keppler emphasized in a most memorable speech,[14] are symptoms of a sickness which, when they occur in overwhelming numbers, is not the cause of a nation's downfall, but a warning of it. Of course, it lies in the nature of this sin, as in all evil, that it should bring forth more sin. By undermining the will and raising barriers against the intervention of divine grace, it is bound to produce more evil. But the priest who, in cases of sexual trespass, concentrates the attention wholly upon the sin is like a doctor who treats a boil by putting a plaster on it, without paying any close attention to the real seat of the trouble—the poison in the blood. There can be no doubt that a whole host of sexual offenses, much premature erotic excitement among the young, and much abuse of marriage are due to the housing shortage. The war, political confusion, the problem of displaced persons, and the steady increase in divorce are having a disruptive effect upon family life and producing conditions favorable to "free love." Add to this the monotony of factory work which induces undue fatigue, and you have a very likely explanation for the irresistible impulse which drives many wage slaves to seek a stimulus, so vividly suggested by films and other modern types of amusements, in erotic adventures. The more a priest and his parishoners unite in a campaign against social evils, the more successful they will be in stopping this erotic trend. But the priest's progress in this direction will depend on the extent to which he is able to awaken the sense of mutual justice and love in the souls under his care. What is needed is that sense of brotherhood and solidarity that animated the early Christian communities. Then, practice will substantiate the theory of the primacy of love. The priest who succeeds in keeping attention fixed on God's highest commandment and on the need for brotherly love, preaching these as often and as impressively as the Good Shepherd did, will do far more to exterminate prostitution than one who launches frequent philippics against the abuse of marriage. When all the members of a parish—laborers and peasants, landowners, merchants, and professional men—are united in full consciousness of their unity as members of Christ's Church, branches of the Vine, enjoying not only the same privileges, but also sharing the same responsibilities, there will be little trespass against chastity or modesty. The priest who can claim to have awakened such a spirit among his parishioners is unlikely to be outdone by one who preaches only to rail against fashions, amusements, and the frivolities of the age. Moreover, if he should find it necessary on rare occasions to say a few serious words about sexual offenses, he will be sure to have the majority of his parishoners solidly behind him.

Perhaps there was some justification for the charge often brought by what used to be called the "proletariat," namely, that in the past, the important matters of social justice and love were not stressed nearly as much in our pulpits as were the other moral commandments, particularly the Sixth. The great Keppler's was a voice in the wilderness, and his fiercest opponents were to be found in the ranks of those who should have stood by him. The great workers' pope, Leo XIII, was also misunderstood in his own times; he, more than any other, was the man who drew attention to the social problems facing Christendom and the crying need for solutions which could only be found in the Christian requirements of equality and brotherly love. If once that spirit of love which our Saviour described as the sign by which His disciples would be known, and which indeed was the pride of the early Christian communities, could be recognized again as the greatest of all commandments and honored as such, there would not only be an end of all social problems, but every other moral law would gain by it, not least among them the Sixth Commandment. *Caritas* is the cardinal factor beside which all other questions, no matter how important they may be, must take a back seat.

In this respect, of course, the example set by the priest himself is of paramount importance. Of what use are all his thunderbolts from the pulpit about "immorality" if he lives in disharmony with his parishoners, shows little sympathy for their woes and worries, disagrees with his curates, quarrels with neighboring priests, and makes himself unpopular generally? It would be far better if he kept silent about "morality" for, in truth, his own behavior is far more immoral than the trespasses against which he protests. We priests are proud of our vocation, and take a very poor view of those who, by their failings, bring the whole priesthood into disrepute. Generally speaking, the Catholic clergy are respected for their high standard of *castitas*—but it would be a great pity if the same did not apply to our brotherly love! If *caritas* is the supreme virtue, it accords just as little with morality and good repute for the clergy to be antagonistic, envious, spiteful, as it would for them to offend against chastity. Surely there is something wrong with a priest's idea of morality if, though extremely anxious to avoid any temptation of the flesh, he finds his conscience by no means unduly troubled if he falls into the sin of pride or self-righteousness, or quarrels with his parish through unyielding self-assertion.

It is equally important for him to foster this spirit of love among those who listen attentively to his admonitions from the pulpit. Sometimes the very people who attend church most regularly, who never miss the sacraments, who belong to all the guilds and brotherhoods, are quarrelsome among themselves and very prone to spiteful rivalry. This should not be. That well-known type, the "praying sisterhood" for whom Abraham a Sancta Clara coined the apt description "angelus in ecclesia, diabolus in casa" (angel in church and devil at home), does more harm to the cause of true piety and morality than an open enemy—for there is always a chance that the unbeliever may be converted, while the hypocrite gives scoffers continual cause to suspect and ridicule piety. This is the type of devotee who will always most readily applaud attacks on fashions, dances, movies, theaters, and so on—but who is very ready to take offense if the priest points out that all prayers and all piety without love are tinkling cymbals; that chastity without love is sterile (Augustine), a lamp without oil (Bernard); that diligent reception of the sacraments, if combined with hatred of family and neighbors, is actually sacrilege. "And if any man think himself to be religious, not bridling his tongue but deceiving his own heart, this man's religion is vain. Religion clean and undefiled before God and the Father is this: to visit the fatherless and widows in their tribulation and to keep oneself unspotted from this world" (Jas. 1:26-27).

Certainly the teaching of the primacy of love has never been denied in theory; but, in practice, the necessary consequence is not always drawn. A considerable loss to the effectiveness of our preaching has been caused by changes in the values of words—changes which have succeeded in establishing themselves in the language since the Great Schism, and have found acceptance, not only among the uneducated public, but also in our schools and our pulpits. The use of the word immoral in the sense of unchaste has completely unbalanced the concept of morality; and this has been further accentuated by a biased rigor brought to bear on offenses against chastity. Until a more exact use of words becomes compulsory, we must see to it that the consequences of this misuse are at least counteracted. That can only be brought about by taking extra care, on the one hand, that we ourselves do not stray into thought processes which depart from the sound principles of moral theology and, on the other hand, that we take extra care to stress the love of God and of our neighbor as the true foundation on which all morality must be based. By this we shall certainly not relegate chastity to a minor position, or treat sins against it with indifference; but *caritas* will be given its proper place as the primary virtue, the one from which all others spring and take on extra luster.

Year by year, complaints are made in religious circles about the mounting tide of unnatural eroticism in films, novels, popular songs, and periodicals. Unfortunately, these complaints are fully justified. They must be regarded as signposts to the decay of modern civilization. But it would not be right to turn a deaf ear to the cry for true love which somehow asserts itself above all this seeming tumult. It is this true love which mankind needs, more perhaps today than ever before. Because it cannot find this love, the world seeks for substitutes in dangerous and forbidden ways. The yearning for love is the strongest hunger of the human heart, and God Himself has placed that yearning there in order that it may prove an irresistible stimulus, driving man to the ultimate purpose of his existence—unity with the inexhaustible love of God. All great leaders of men have been driven on by this yearning. All the great cultural periods of the various races have reached their peak through this mighty urge; it has resulted in lofty cathedrals, in undying verse—in a striving for the one eternal love which has always been the ultimate goal, even when those who were driven on did not fully recognize it. Where this yearning ceases, all is barren; hunger, hatred, and loneliness fill the soul. The most frightening prophecy our Lord ever made was not that, in the last days of this age, people would wage war on one another, that false prophets would arise, or that the stars would fall from the firmament—no, the most terrible fate of all is reflected in the words: "the charity of many shall grow cold" (Matt. 24:12). How icily cold the world would be without love! If love should ever cease, then indeed man would be a slave, a mere number, a robot in a vast machine. Of what use would it be then to have miracles of technique and super-department stores? All the great discoveries of science, of which we are justly proud, are perhaps destined to be destroyed by a future atomic bomb—because the world has lost the gift of love! Of what use is a highly developed intelligence if tyranny wields the scepter and ruthlessness proclaims its mastery over all? The whole world, if uncharitableness triumphs, can become one vast battlefield in which men study, by the most refined inventions, only how best to destroy all that has been built up by creative artists and poets for century after century. Then, indeed, the world will be sick unto death—a world bereft of love.

It is the preacher's most exalted task to make the sick world aware of the means by which it can be healed, and never to cease reiterating these good tidings. The only true healing agent is love. Christ our Lord mentions love as the first and most important sign by which men will recognize His disciples. The apostles join in proclaiming that love was the most distinct characteristic of the early Christian communities. Ignatius of Antioch defines the early Church as "the bond of love." Woe to any present-day preacher who ever forgets this truth!

NOTES

1. *Scholastik, loc. cit.*
2. *Allgemeine Rundshau,* 43 (1932).
3. *Theologia moralis, lib.* IV *de sexto,* no. 413.
4. "Sermons on the Ten Commandments." [Available in German and French, originally published in Hungarian.—Ed.]
5. A. Groeteken, O.F.M., *Dietrich Koelde* (Kevelaer, 1935), p. 143.
6. St. Bernard, *De conversione ad clericos,* chap. 5.
7. Cf. Göbel edition, *op. cit.,* sermon on sin, p. 92; no. 17, on peace, p. 267; no. 19, on the Ten Commandments, p. 307.
8. Ferel-Fetscher, *loc. cit.,* pp. 369 and 376.
9. Homily 12 on the Epistle to the Colossians; cf. Gatterer-Krus, *Die Erzeihung zur Keuschheit* (Innsbruck, 1911), pp. 10 and 98, note.
10. *Jugend, loc. cit.*
11. See J. Müller, *loc. cit.,* p. 56.
12. See the instructive work of Dr. Rötheli in Hornstein-Faller, *op. cit.,* p. 180; also Frederich von Gagern, *Seelenleben und Seelenführung,* published as vol. IV of *Die Zeit der Geschlechtlichen Reife* (Frankfort on the Main, 1951).
13. Göbel edition, *op. cit.,* p. 305.
14. In *Wasser aus dem Felzen,* I (Freiburg, 1927), 324.

Index

Index

B

Index

Index

Index

Index

Index

Index

H-I

J-K

Index

Index

Index

Index

R

Index

Index

T

U-V

A NOTE ON THE TYPE

IN WHICH THIS BOOK IS SET

This book is set in Garamond, a type face considered by many as one of the most successful ever introduced. Claude Garamond, the designer of these beautiful types, was a pupil of Geoffroy Tory, a leader of the Renaissance in France, a university professor, artist, designer and printer who set out to place French on an equal footing with Latin and Greek as a language of culture. Garamond's evenness of color throughout the font is highly appreciated by book designers. The moderately strong fine lines tend to soften the effect, which is decidedly agreeable to many. This book was composed by Wickersham Printing Company, Lancaster, Pa., and bound by Moore & Company of Baltimore. The typography and design of this book are by Howard N. King.